Gathering Together Volume 2: Christian Testimony

Gathering Together Volume 2: Christian Testimony

Lance Lambert

LANCE LAMBERT MINISTRIES

Richmond, Virginia, USA

ISBN: 978-1-68389-019-5

www.lancelambert.org

Printed in the United States of America

Contents

Introduction

The content of these pages, "Christian Testimony," is the transcription of six messages given in 1968 by Lance Lambert. During that time he gave a series of twelve messages to Christians meeting together at Halford House, Richmond, England under the title Meeting Together. The previous six messages have been published as "Volume One: Christian Fellowship" and are also available from Lance Lambert Ministries.

The emphasis of this current volume is from a phrase oft repeated in the Book of Revelation: the testimony of Jesus.

"John bore witness to the word of God and the testimony of Jesus." (Revelation 1:2).

"The testimony of Jesus is the spirit of prophecy" (Revelation 19:10b).

What is the testimony of Jesus? Is it possible to see its practical expression on earth in our day? What is the vessel for holding the testimony of Jesus? What is the key to the recovery of the testimony of Jesus? Truly, in our day and time, understanding the testimony of Jesus is of vital importance.

As Lance prayed: "Beloved Lord, make us those who in our hearts really understand what the testimony [of Jesus] is and may we be those who hold it."

1.
The Local Church

We will begin with five series of scriptures regarding the church:

1. The Church: Its Universal Nature

The first series of scriptures is on "the church" on earth in its universal nature through the generations of this age.

Matthew 16:18
And I also say unto thee, that thou art Peter, and upon this rock I will build my church; and the gates of Hell shall not prevail against it.

1 Corinthians 12:28a
And God hath set some in the church.

Galatians 1:13
For ye have heard of my manner of life in time past in the Jews'

religion, how that beyond measure I persecuted the church of God, and made havoc of it.

Ephesians 1:22
And he put all things in subjection under his feet, and gave him to be head over all things to the church.

Ephesians 3:10
To the intent that now unto the principalities and the powers in the heavenly places might be made known through the church the manifold wisdom of God.

Ephesians 5:23–25, 32
Christ also loved the church and gave himself up for it ...
This mystery is great: but I speak of Christ and of the church.

(This is all about marriage and what it symbolises, what it signifies. Again and again we find the word "the church." It is *the* church that is in view there.)

Colossians 1:18a, 24
And he is the head of the body, the church ... Now I rejoice in my sufferings for your sake, and fill up on my part that which is lacking of the afflictions of Christ in my flesh for his body's sake, which is the church.

1 Timothy 3:15a
But if I tarry long, that thou mayest know how men ought to behave

themselves in the house of God, which is the church of the living God.

2. The Churches:

The second series is on this term "the churches," and the actual word "churches" is used approximately thirty-five times in the New Testament.

Acts 14:23

And when they had appointed for them elders in every church (plural).

Acts 15:41

And he went through Syria and Cilicia, confirming the churches.

Acts 16:5

So the churches were strengthened in the faith, and increased in number daily.

Romans 16:4, 16

Who for my life laid down their own necks; unto whom not only I give thanks, but also all the churches of the Gentiles ... Salute one another with a holy kiss. All the churches of Christ salute you.

1 Corinthians 7:17

Only, as the Lord hath distributed to each man, as God hath called each, so let him walk. And so ordain I in all the churches.

I Corinthians 11:16

But if any man seemeth to be contentious, we have no such custom, neither the churches of God.

I Corinthians 16:1, 19

Now concerning the collection for the saints, as I gave order to the churches of Galatia, so also do ye ... The churches of Asia salute you.

II Corinthians 8:1, 18–19, 23–24

Moreover, brethren, we make known to you the grace of God which hath been given in the churches of Macedonia ... And we have sent together with him the brother whose praise in the gospel is spread through all the churches; and not only so, but who was also appointed by the churches to travel with us in the matter of this grace ... Whether any inquire about Titus, he is my partner and fellow-worker to you-ward, or our brethren, they are the apostles of the churches, they are the glory of Christ. Show ye therefore unto them in the face of the churches the proof of your love, and of our glorying on your behalf.

Galatians 1:2, 22–23a

And all the brethren that are with me, unto the churches of Galatia ... And I was still unknown by face unto the churches of Judea which were in Christ: but they only heard say, He that once persecuted us now preacheth the faith.

1 Thessalonians 2:14

For ye, brethren, became imitators of the churches of God which are in Judea in Christ Jesus.

Revelation 22:16

I Jesus have sent mine angel to testify unto you these things for the churches.

(This is very interesting because the whole book of the Revelation as we call it, the apocalypse, was given for *the churches*.)

3. The Church at:

Acts 11:22

And the report concerning them came to the ears of the church which was in Jerusalem.

Acts 13:1a

Now there were at Antioch, in the church that was there.

Romans 16:1

I commend unto you Phoebe our sister, who is a servant of the church that is at Cenchreæ.

1 Corinthians 1:2

Unto the church of God which is at Corinth.

4. Revelation 1–3 Revealing the Church Universal, the Church *in,* and the Church *at*

The fourth series is all to do with the first three chapters of Revelation. We have the three things we talked about here. First of all is the church in its *totality.* In a sense, it is the church on earth through the centuries and generations of this age. There are seven churches selected. You must all realise that the Lord could have sent a message to every church existing at that time. There were thousands and thousands of churches. Why did the Lord choose seven? Why not choose twelve? Why not choose nine? Why not choose four? Why choose seven? Most of you know that numbers have symbolic value in the Bible, in the Old Testament especially, but of course in the New Testament also because it was a Jewish way of doing things. The figure seven is the symbol for totality, completeness, fullness, everything there—seven days of the week—absolutely complete. Therefore, you have seven churches selected from the province of Asia, and these seven are selected to represent the totality of the church, the church in completeness, the church in its fullness in time on earth.

Someone might ask straightaway: "How do you know that?" Someone else says, "I am not sure about that; surely there were literally seven churches." Of course there were literally seven churches; we know that. But the fact that seven were selected, the accent is not on the literalness of the seven but on the symbolic value of the seven.

Revelation 3:1b

These things saith he that hath the seven Spirits of God.

We all know that it would be an absolute blasphemous heresy to teach that God has seven Spirits. God has only one Spirit—God the Father, God the Son and God the Holy Spirit—Three in One and One in Three. But the seven Spirits of God are the Holy Spirit in all His fullness indwelling the seven churches. That is the glory of it. Just as there is only one church, there is only one Christ, so there is only one Holy Spirit. But the one church is divided into seven here, and the one Holy Spirit is divided into seven in this sense.

Revelation 1:10–13

I was in the Spirit on the Lord's day, and I heard behind me a great voice, as of a trumpet saying, What thou seest, write in a book and send it to the seven churches: unto Ephesus, and unto Smyrna, and unto Pergamum, and unto Thyatira, and unto Sardis, and unto Philadelphia, and unto Laodicea. And I turned to see the voice that spake with me. And having turned I saw seven golden candlesticks; and in the midst of the candlesticks one like unto a son of man, clothed with a garment down to the foot, and girt about at the breasts with a golden girdle.

If you look further down it is the Lord Jesus who is in the midst of the seven churches. It is a picture of the church in its completeness and fullness in time with the Lord; the presence of God walking in the midst of the seven.

Then you have the churches:

Revelation 2:7, 11

He that hath an ear, let him hear what the Spirit saith to the churches.

This word is found again in verses 17 and 29; and chapter 3 verses 6, 13 and 22. Why did the Lord not say, "He that hath an ear, let him hear what the Spirit says to the church?" But He did not say that, for instance, when speaking to the church at Ephesus; it says to "the churches."

Then there is "the church in."

Revelation 2:1, 8, 12, 18

To the angel of the church in Ephesus ...
To the angel of the church in Smyrna ...
To the angel of the church in Pergamum ...
To the angel of the church in Thyatira ...

Revelation 3:1, 7, 14

To the church in ..."

Here are three things—first the church in its universal nature in one sense. It is the incorruptible thing represented by the golden lampstand.

Then you have the church in time and on earth.

Then you have the church at, the church divided by geographical locality—only one church divided by no other division than where the believers happen to live.

5. The Church as the Bride and the City of God

There is one other series of scriptures having to do with the church as "the bride" and "city of God."

In Revelation 21:2, 9 and 10: the bride and the city are linked up as being synonymous.

In Hebrews 12:22–23: the city is the church of the firstborn.

In Ephesians 5:23–25 it is the bride who is the church.

Compare that with Revelation 22:16: "I Jesus have sent mine angel to testify unto you these things for the churches," and Revelation chapters 1–3. In other words, the whole book of Revelation is to be seen against the context of the church and the churches. You must understand it like that. If you do not, you fail to understand it. The Lord's last words were, "I Jesus have sent mine angel to testify unto you these things for the churches."

Then the very next word is: "The Spirit and the bride say, Come." The churches and the bride are linked together. Now you will find it again in these first three chapters also: "He that overcometh." The message to every one of the seven churches in the first three chapters of Revelation ends with this clarion challenge or call: He that overcometh shall inherit this or that or the other. Seven times the Lord says that. At the end of Revelation 21:7 we find that the city of God, the New Jerusalem, the bride is linked to the overcoming in the churches, for it says, "He that overcometh shall inherit all these things." In order to be in the bride of God, and part of the bride of God, part of the city of God, one has to overcome within the sphere of the churches.

God's Method of Expressing the Church to the World

I am going to launch straightway into the next point that I want to make in these studies: Why are you at Halford House? (The other points are in *Gathering Together Volume 1*.) It is this: God's one and only method of expressing the church, the body of Christ to the world is the local church. I will repeat that again: God's one and only method of expressing the church, the body of Christ to this world is the local church. There are two terms which are used frequently in the New Testament. The first is the church and the second is the churches. These two terms are found again and again, and we have read through quite a number of them. We have not exhausted them all by any means, but have just selected a certain number.

The Church

When the term *the church* is used, (you have to understand it by the context) it speaks always of the body of Christ universal, world-wide, those still on earth, and those already gathered in the glory. It is a term that covers all ages, all parts and times, climes and peoples. In this present age, and indeed all the ages of time, it is invisible and intangible. I want to say that clearly. It is *the church* of God eternal, indestructible, indivisible and glorious.

The Churches

Then you have another term, *the churches*, and this term speaks always of *the church* in its practical expression on earth. It is the church tangible, visible, concretely expressed in time on this earth in a given locality or given localities; all that is meant by the term *the church* expressed and manifested locally. Does that not lift this horrible little term, the local church, onto another level altogether? That is God's idea that the local church is not something petty, something sordid, something just earthly. God's idea in the local church is that it is there alone that everything in the eternal church is to be expressed, or if you like, it is to be obtained as well as expressed. The principles that govern the eternal are to operate in the local. It is as simple as that.

Before we can actually come to the point in this, it is important to recognise that the churches are *the* one church represented and expressed in different places. I want to make that point very, very clearly. It is the *one* church. There is only *one* church. The church is not the aggregate of churches; it is not the sum total of so many churches. Look at it the other way round. The churches are *the* church expressed. Now you have it. You must not look at it the other way. You must see that the churches are the one church expressed in all the different places on the earth.

The Church in Time and on Earth

Acts 15:3a says: "They therefore, being brought on their way by the church, passed through both Phoenicia and Samaria, declaring the conversion of the Gentiles." Now we might well ask, "What is this term, *the church*?" because it is not a particular church; yet it is the church in time and on earth in localities. It is only one church, so all the way through Phoenicia and Samaria they went from church to church to church. But Dr. Luke puts it like this: "It was the church that brought them on." There is only one church, not lots of different churches. There is only one church expressed in the different places, so he puts it very simply: "the church brought them on."

We find it again in Acts 9:31a, and there is a very real difference in the translations of the Revised Version, the American Standard Version, the Revised Standard Version and the New English Bible to the Authorised King James Version. This is the Revised Standard Version: "So the church throughout all Judea and Galilee and Samaria had peace." It is never the church *of* Judea and Samaria. It is always *the* church throughout. In other words, only one church is expressed in all these churches throughout this area. It is only one church divided into these places.

Corinthians 1:2: "Unto the church of God which is at Corinth, even them that are sanctified in Christ Jesus, called to be saints, with all that call upon the name of our Lord Jesus Christ in every place, their Lord and ours."

It is only one church. It just so happens that the believers at Corinth were in the church of God which is at Corinth, but they were actually one with all those who call upon the name of our Lord Jesus in every place with all the other churches. It is only one church.

The Oneness of Christ

This simple fact that governs the division of the church on earth into churches is the absolute oneness of Christ. He is absolutely one. There are not lots of Christs; there is only one Christ. He is indivisible. There is only one Christ and this simple fact absolutely governs the division of the church into churches. Since Christ is everything in the church, He is all in the church, all and in all; therefore, it is one body, one Christ. Then, whether it is Jerusalem, Caesarea, Antioch, Thessalonica, Rome, Philippi, or Richmond, Oslo, New York, Shanghai, it is only one Christ. There is not a different Christ in Tokyo to the Christ here in Richmond. There was not a different Christ in Thessalonica to the Christ in Jerusalem. He was precisely the same Christ. There was not a different body of Christ in Rome to the one that was in Thessalonica. There is only one body because there is only one Christ—one Christ, one body. So if it is the one body in Rome, it is the same body in Jerusalem, the same body in Antioch, the same body in Ephesus, and it is the same body in Richmond, thank God, all these years later. It is the same body in Tokyo; it is the same body in Shanghai, it is the same body in Oslo. It does not matter where you are; it is the same *one* Christ. Nevertheless, because of our obvious, physical limitation we cannot all assemble in one place. I think that is obvious to everyone, and there is therefore the need to do something.

Assembling Together in Geographical Locality

The Scripture says in Hebrews 10:24–25: "We are to provoke one another unto love." (That is a very strong word.) "Not forsaking the assembling of yourselves together as the manner of some is, and so much the more as you see that day approaching." In other words, the nearer that day comes the more careful we ought to be about the assembling of ourselves together. How can we all assemble together? We are only one church, but we cannot all assemble in one place, can we? It would be absolutely ridiculous if the millions and millions of Christians were all somehow to come together; and if we did all come together what would we do? We could not all get into one building. So because of the obvious, physical limitation the Holy Spirit has seen fit to divide the church by only one means and that is locality, into geographical locality. He divides the church with the minimum division where you live, where you are resident. It is quite simple.

The Church Gathers for Mutual Building up

There is a need for us to assemble together for mutual building up. How can a million Christians build one another up? We can listen to Billy Graham, but how can we build one another up in such a meeting? For mutual building up there has to be some kind of fragmentation, some kind of breaking up of things into smaller units so that there is a workable unity in which everyone can build one another up, where there can be interchange and intercourse spiritually, where there can be true fellowship. Otherwise, everything will be abstract and vague.

The Church Gathers for Prayer and Executive Action

We can all talk about the most wonderful and blessed fellowship when a million Christians gather together—and so it would be marvellous and wonderful. We had a taste of this recently at Earls Court when thousands came together there, but that must remain very vague and abstract. Believe me, we can escape all kinds of issues in that kind of fellowship. Therefore, there is a need for mutual building up of one another; there is a need for prayer, for executive prayer, and executive action. How can we pray an executive prayer if there are a million of us? We cannot get down to the business if we have a prayer meeting with a million people in attendance. It is marvellous and wonderful, but it is not practical. Why? Because we do not yet have glorified bodies. Up there it will all be different, but down here we are in a different dimension and we have to recognize this physical limitation. The human mind is not made to be able to take in millions of people in a prayer meeting. It is an intensely practical matter that we are talking about.

Not only that, how can millions of people take executive action, rising up together and really hitting on the head some sickness or illness or something else, some bondage? Of course, they could do it, but they would have to spend all their time doing it. They would not have time for anything else if everyone had to bring it to a central authority in the million for the whole lot to hear. Everything would become absolutely unwieldy like a bureaucratic state. Of course, God is not a bureaucrat; that is the glory of it.

The Church Gathers for Witness, Service and Discipline

Then again you and I need to be able to meet together for witness and service, not just to be lost in a huge crowd. "Ye shall be witnesses unto Me." We are priests to serve the Lord.

Then, of course, there is the matter of discipline. If we were all to meet together in this huge number, I think the elders would be in eternal session disciplining people. It is impossible! Now I have spent a little time being almost childlike because this whole matter is absolute simplicity. For facility, purely and merely for practical government, for practical order, for practical discipline, for practical experience corporately of all the church meetings, the church is divided into geographical localities.

Matthew 16:18: "Upon this rock I will build my church." Here is the church worldwide, universal, those in glory already, those on earth in every clime and every part of the age.

Now turn over the pages to chapter 18:15–17a: "And if thy brother sin against thee." How can you bring a matter like this to that church in Matthew 16? There is no brother that sins in that one. "If thy brother sin against thee, go, show him his fault between thee and him alone: if he hear thee, thou hast gained thy brother. But if he hear thee not, take with thee one or two more, that at the mouth of two witnesses or three every word may be established. And if he refuse to hear them, tell it unto the church also."

Do you know what that means? It means that somewhere or other the church—the church Jesus is building upon this rock—has to be concretely expressed in some locality. Let me tell you this: however we fail in that church, expressed in time and in locality, when a person brings a matter to that church, the whole eternal church is involved. It is as simple as that. We cannot make any division. That is why the apostle Paul could say, "I am there in my spirit, I judge the man" (see 1 Corinthians 5:3). He was not even at Corinth but he said, "I am there." The whole lot is there because it is the church.

How can you bring a matter to the church if there is no such thing as it being broken up into something that we call geographical localities? Here is the wisdom of God. Make no mistake about it. It is absolute divine wisdom. Oh, the Lord is the Master at understanding the devious ways of our hearts. Devious they are. He understands us back to front and top to bottom, and He understands what lies in the deepest depth of our being that we do not even know or understand. The Spirit of God searches it all and He knows all about it, and in His wisdom He has trapped us. Anyone who tries to get out of this trap woe betide them because however spiritual they may appear to be, much of it is artificial and will one day be shown up to be so. The Lord has wisdom in this matter.

What does this all mean? If we go on here it says, "Tell it unto the church: and if he refuse to hear the church also, let him be unto thee as the Gentile and the publican. Verily I say unto you, What things soever ye shall bind on earth shall be bound in heaven" (Matthew 18:17b–18a). The church in heaven says, "Ratify it." If a church on earth in locality says, "This thing is bound, the church in glory says, "Amen; it is done." We are one. "Whatsoever things ye shall loose on earth shall be loosed in heaven" (v.18b). It is one church. Glorious! In our business meetings Abraham, Isaac, and Jacob are actually watching. It is quite remarkable, but they are all there. We do not know if they will ask us any questions one day, but the whole set in ranks of the saints, the church of the firstborn, are all involved in it all because we are only one church. We just happen to be here in 1968 in Richmond, but the thing goes right back to when the God of glory first appeared to our father Abraham. That is where it all began. Of course, the full glory of revelation of the mystery of the body of Christ was only given after Pentecost. But we must be careful of digressing.

There is Only One Church

Let me put it another way. If I had lived in Ephesus then I would have been in the church at Ephesus. If I had lived in Thyatira I would have been in the church at Thyatira. If I had lived in Rome I would have been in the church at Rome. It was only one church, the same church. It just so happened that where I lived, that is where I was in the church. It was really the church of God, but it was the church of God at Rome, the church of God at Ephesus, or the church of God at Thyatira. If I live in Richmond I am in the church of God which is at Richmond.

I have asked you this question before: To which church did the apostle Paul belong? The fact of the matter is he belonged to the church. When he was in Ephesus, he was in the church at Ephesus. When he was in Thessalonica, he was in the church at Thessalonica. When he was in Antioch, he was in the church at Antioch. He was not a member of the church at Antioch on missionary work. There is only one church. When I am in an aircraft, I am just in the church. It is as simple as that if it brings it home to you. It seems a bit stupid, but if it brings the truth of the whole thing home to you, I am glad.

There were never two churches in one locality. It was always the church at Antioch, the church at Ephesus, the church at Philadelphia, and so on. Never do we read of the churches at Antioch or the churches at Philadelphia. Even when the believers in Jerusalem numbered thousands and thousands and there was no adequate central meeting place to house them all, it was still the church which was at Jerusalem. I would like to show you this to prove it to you because people say, "We are living in the twentieth century. If you brought everyone together in such and such a place there would be thousands and thousands of them." In this particular instance it is a New Testament problem.

Acts 8:1a: "And there arose on that day a great persecution against the church which was in Jerusalem." This was the church which was at Jerusalem. Now someone says, "Now I've got you." There was tremendous persecution and they were all scattered all over the place. But it was still the church of God which was at Jerusalem before that persecution took place because it says, "There arose persecution."

Acts 2:41, 46: "They then that received his word were baptized: and there were added unto them in that day about three thousand souls. And they continued stedfastly in the apostles' teaching and fellowship, in the breaking of bread and the prayers ... And day by day, continuing stedfastly with one accord in the temple." (There is the central meeting place in the temple, which was not a very sympathetic place. Every day they met in the temple to fellowship together, the whole lot of them.) "And breaking bread at home, they took their food with gladness and singleness of heart." They broke bread, the Lord's table, from home to home in all the areas around.

Acts 4:4: "But many of them that heard the word believed; and the number of the men came to be about five thousand." If we counted the ladies, there must have been ten thousand of them. I am going by New Testament procedure and not by the common thing now of three or four or five ladies to every man among Christian places. So just at the minimum there would have been ten thousand.

Acts 6:7: "And the word of God increased; and the number of the disciples multiplied in Jerusalem exceedingly; and a great company of the priests were obedient to the faith."

Acts 8:1b: "The church which was in Jerusalem." Now there must have been something like twelve or fifteen thousand believers in Jerusalem until the persecution scattered the majority of them which left a much smaller group still numbering some thousands. Is it not an interesting fact that it was never at any time called the churches which are at Jerusalem, but always throughout the whole of the New Testament it is always called *the* church which is at Jerusalem.

The Church in a Home

Then someone will bring up the references to: "the church which is in your house" or "the church which is in their house." There are only three of them—1 Corinthians 16:19, Romans 16:5, Colossians 4:15.

People will immediately bring this up and say, "But surely this destroys the whole thing." But it does not at all. First of all, you will note that one of the places mentioned is Ephesus. Aquila and Priscilla were wealthy people. Today we would call them factory owners; they had a tent making business. Evidently they had a big home in which they probably had a very large area for making carpets and tents and saddles because tent makers were carpet makers as well as saddle makers. It was a very big business. Therefore they may well have met in a very large area, we do not know. In the reference in I Corinthians 16:19 you will see that Paul sent the greetings of the church which was in their house. Now it could easily, conceivably be the church which was at Ephesus at that point that was still meeting in Aquila and Priscilla's home because it could have held the church there. So that does not invalidate the argument at all.

One of the other two references is the Roman one, and again it is Aquila and Priscilla, a most extraordinary couple—husband and wife. They were the two, by the way, who took Apollos aside and instructed him more fully in the way. They had gone off to Rome now and they had another big home there. People say this shows that the church which was at Rome must have numbered many more than could get in their home. Two points about this: first it does not say that Aquila and Priscilla were actually resident in Rome. It could easily have been in a place outside of Rome for Rome was the main metropolis of the day. On the other hand, even if it had been so, Rome was the biggest city in the old world numbering about a million people, roughly the size of Copenhagen today. The fact is that even if the church had been split up into four or five or six groups it would still have been the church which is in your house. Supposing I had written from Jerusalem. I might have said, "The church of Jerusalem, meeting in so and so's house, sends greetings." It does not mean that the whole church in Jerusalem, numbering twelve thousand, were managing to get into sister so and so's house. It just means that in that particular district all the believers were meeting in her home. It does not invalidate the argument at all.

The other reference in Colossians is to Laodicea and Nymphas, or as you will see in the margin, Nympha, another lady. (Nympha is a lady, Nymphas is a gentleman, a brother.) It says "and the church which is in their house," or in the margin, her house; we are not quite sure. It could be the church which was at Laodicea which was meeting in Nympha's house, or it could be that there was somewhere else that Paul was referring to in another smaller place. We do not know; but what we can say is that it does not invalidate what we have said.

The Churches, Plural

I think we ought to note another point in this matter. Whenever the plural, "churches" is used, it is always used of an area or a region consisting of a number of towns or villages and never of one city. We never, at any single place in the whole New Testament, read of the churches at Rome, the churches at Thessalonica, the churches at Athens, the churches at Alexandria or anywhere like that.

We do read of, for instance, I Corinthians 16:1: The churches of Galatia." I Corinthians 16:19: "The churches of Asia." II Corinthians 8:1: "The churches of Macedonia." Galatians 1:22: "The churches of Judea." We could go on. The plural is always associated with areas or regions in which there are a number of localities. I personally believe this matter is the simplest, most rational matter, in one way, in Scripture. I am therefore amazed that there is not a greater clarity amongst Christians on this matter. It is quite extraordinary the sheer, absolute, blindness that there is when it comes to this simple, rational matter.

What is Locality?

Let me say it again: the only division of the church recognized and allowed by God in the Scriptures is geographical. That is locality.

1 Corinthians 1:1–2: "... the church of God which is at Corinth." Compare that, the church of God which is at Corinth with Titus 1:5: "For this cause left I thee in Crete, that thou shouldest set in order the things that were wanting, and appoint elders in every city." Don't you think that is extraordinary that the apostle Paul did not say, "And to appoint elders in every church"? But he does not. He said, "Appoint elders in every city."

In Acts 14:23a we have precisely the same phrase put this way: "And when they had appointed for them elders in every church." It seems clear to me that the church is synonymous with the locality, with the city.

That leads me to this question. What do we mean by locality? We will answer in this way. It would seem from Scripture that it was an administrative unit. It is simple as that. It was not a regional or a national unit, but it was a local administrative unit. In other words, civil authority is recognized in this matter. Where there is Philippi, a definite civil administrative unit, or Ephesus, a civil administrative unit, or Jerusalem, a civil administrative unit, that is recognized as a locality.

Obviously, in New Testament times the matter was far, far simpler because localities were defined. There was none of this highly urbanized society in which we live. Even Rome, which was the greatest of all, was nothing like anything we know today. They, for instance, did not face the problem being presented to them of a huge area where one town had spread and spread and swallowed up a whole number of others such as London. You can read books that speak of going by horse through meadows and fields from Richmond right the way up to St. Martin-in-the-Fields. The city began further on—that was Westminster. Those in the New Testament did not face this problem of highly urbanised areas, such as New York, Los Angeles or Tokyo, which have somehow grown and swallowed up a whole number of places.

Nevertheless, let us say this: the principle holds good in general. In such cases, as we just mentioned, London and other places like that, the people of God must seek the Lord's mind as to how this principle applies. We are not to put it aside. It is not right to put aside any principle, but to seek the mind of God as to how it applies in our twentieth century condition. There are exceptions, of course, to the rule, and we have to face that, but we cannot be too dogmatic in stating that any division of the church other than the geographical one into localities is not of God and must result in disruption and disintegration. Therefore, anything that calls itself a church which covers less than a locality is not a church, and anything which is more than the locality is not a church either. It is a work.

The Foundation of the Church—
Jesus Christ Alone

The foundation upon which a church is built is Jesus Christ alone. That is the foundation; there is no other foundation. We do not build on history or tradition, however marvellous. Nor do we build on teaching as such, nor even experiences as such. We build upon the foundation which is Jesus Christ and Him alone.

However, this matter of the foundation being Jesus Christ is neither abstract nor vague. It is absolutely concrete for it is the foundation which is Jesus Christ alone as found in that particular locality. I cannot stress that fervently or vehemently enough. It is the first fundamental in the practical outworking of the church. Until the Holy Spirit finds such a recognition on our part as to this matter of the foundation being Jesus Christ as found in our locality, He will not commit Himself to corporate building work under any circumstances whatsoever. It does not matter where you go in the whole world, you will not find any building work unless it is on the foundation of Jesus Christ. Now I am not talking about personal building up. I am not talking about personal increase to a measure. I am talking about the actual building together that we read of in the New Testament, which is for most Christians a myth, a legend or a fairy tale. They say, "Marvellous, the primitive church. They had all things in common. They had a belonging, they felt they belonged." It is something that everyone thinks happened in the beginning, but it is a fairy tale, legend, primitive, or prehistoric.

Why doesn't the Holy Spirit commit Himself in this matter of knitting people together, of forming people into one, of causing them to grow up into the Head, of somehow bringing a sense of the whole body? Unless He gets this simple matter of foundation clear, He will not commit Himself. He treats it all as a work and blesses people individually here, there and everywhere.

I am not very old, but what I have seen has been borne out exactly as I have said in the little I have experienced. It does not matter how great a vision there is, how far people have gone, if this simple matter of Christ as the only foundation in a particular locality is not recognized the Holy Spirit will not commit Himself. That is why there is such a dearth of church building even where the headship of Christ is known to a certain degree. The Lord has to lead us to this matter.

The Vital Importance of the Local Church

This matter of the local church is vitally important because it is the only way God has ordained that the church should be and can be expressed to this world. Indeed, it is the only way this world can see Christ in His oneness, His fullness, and His purpose. He will never be seen in the same way in an individual. But when He builds you into the body, there is such a fullness. You cannot explain it. Strangely enough the world touches it and says, "What is different about that crowd?" It is not just the preaching; it is not just the place. There is some mysterious difference they cannot explain. It is the presence of the church.

In John 17:21 the Lord said this: "That they may all be one ... that the world may believe that thou didst send me." Compare that with John 13:34a–35: "A new commandment I give unto you, that ye love one another ... By this shall all men know that ye are my disciples, if ye have love one to another." In other words, it has to be seen. Where is it seen? It is seen in the local church.

Spiritual Things Will Have a Tangible Expression

I want to say one or two hard things here. This spiritual unity in Christ that we have been talking about, the church of God, ought to have visible and tangible expression on this earth in time. That is what we mean by the word churches. Why is it so often held, indeed so generally held among Christians, that spiritual things have no visible expression, no tangible expression? Indeed, it is an extraordinary thing that the more spiritual you are the more it is held. I often hear people, who I am sure have not thought about it, tell us: "the wind bloweth where it listeth" and now here is the sound thereof; it is concrete expression. You do not know where it is coming from or where it is going to, but you hear it and you can feel it. People do not think.

May I ask why God came in the Person of Jesus Christ? Why did He limit Himself to a human body? Was the Lord Jesus a spiritual Man? Was He of heaven? "Of course," you say. Yet He was a Man like you and me; He was a carpenter. He made tools. He wept. He ate. He lived like you and me. He breathed. All this spirituality was concretely expressed in terms of flesh and blood.

The apostle John tried to make a point of it later when he said, "We touched Him, we handled Him, we saw Him, we heard Him" (see 1 John 1:1–3). The eternal life which was with the Father has been given unto us. It is concrete expression. If we were to apply this idea that spiritual things have no concrete expression to conversion, to new spiritual birth, to sanctification (as I fear some do), to godliness, to true faith, that they are sort of invisible, intangible, where would we be? We would be in an utter mess. Why is this so? Because the Scripture says, "By their fruits you shall know them" (see Matthew 7:16).

When a person is converted, we expect to see a change. We know we always see a change. Something happens! They may still be in their old clothes, all unshaved and down and out, but there is a light in their eyes. We all say, "What's happened?"

I remember one lad at a conference. He was introduced to me by a rather overzealous sister expecting that I should give him the gospel, the works, the whole lot. I took one look at this poor bleary-eyed boy and thought: "Oh, what a mistake!" So I looked at him with all the compassion I could stir up and said to him: "If you wish to talk about these things my room is number so and so. Otherwise I should not bother." He went off. I could not possibly have talked with the poor kid, dragged, more or less, by the hair into such a time. However, he came along to some of the meetings. There he was all skewed looking, sort of like he had been on a rugby field, which he played quite regularly, and obviously not a thing was being learnt.

Then, at the Lord's table I noticed a most extraordinary difference. It was not his tie; he didn't have one. It was not his vest which could be seen by all present. It was not his clothes; they were just the same as they were before. But there was something in his very face. I was transfixed. I thought, "Something has happened to that man." So afterwards I went up and asked him: "What has happened?" He had been converted in his room. There was a tangible, visible change. We expect to see such things.

I think all evangelicals would say this. We expect it in this matter of sanctification. Anyone who talks sanctification and there is nothing of it in their life, it is just wind, hot air.

If we cannot apply this idea of spiritual life being vague, abstract, unseen, invisible and intangible to these things, why should we in God's name apply it to the church and to the unity of Christ? We have absolutely no right whatsoever in any way at all. It is true that this oneness of Christ is essentially a spiritual, inward, organic matter, yet it must have concrete visible expression. This is the whole point of the local church. God's one and only method of expressing the church, the body of Christ to this world is the local church. This is the whole point. Everything is applied in very down-to-earth terms and circumstances in the local church. The Holy Spirit is so faithful to bring all the talk about oneness, and victory, and fullness down to earth in the local church and tests it. Sometimes we are almost afraid to open our mouths because it is tested, tested, tested all the time, but thank God for the testing. We lose all that is artificial, all that is pseudo, all that is superficial, all that is taken on from others. We lose it all because everything is applied in the sphere of the local church. Everything is to have its concrete expression; it does not matter what it is.

This is of tremendous importance, for true spirituality is not a matter of abstract theories, unworkable ideals or impractical attitudes; yet that is the general idea of it. This simple geographical division of the church into churches—so utterly rational and so practical in its nature—not only expresses but also preserves the oneness of Christ.

The Unity and Cohesion of the Church

Now let's say this: the unity and cohesion of the church will never be expressed by world-wide movements, or affiliations, or federations or counsels, such as the ecumenical movement, or the World Council of Churches. It will never be expressed by them. It will only ever be expressed by believers in each locality leaving all that divides and all that which is not the local church and never can be, and taking the ground of the body of Christ.

The local church therefore is three things. First it is inclusive, secondly it is representative of Christ, and thirdly it is responsible locally.

The Local Church is Inclusive

First of all, it is inclusive. It covers and includes every born again believer in its locality, whatever their condition. It brings all together in Christ in that place, whatever their race, whatever their nationality, whatever their social class or spiritual measure or understanding. Every one of us who is a child of God, resident within the boundaries of Richmond upon the Thames, belong to the church of God which is in Richmond. There is no question of Danish or Chinese or Malaysian or American. Visitors? If any of the natives of these islands should feel that way you can be sure they have paralyzed the work of the Holy Spirit because the church is not a matter of visitors. The church is the church. It is super-national, super-racial. We are the church. While you are a resident here you are not a Dane or a Norwegian or a Scot or a Welshman or anything else. You are a Christian and you are a member of the body of Christ with as much right to be here as someone who was actually born in Richmond. It cannot be exclusive of anyone who is a child of God except on certain grounds. We have already mentioned them—discipline, apostasy, heresy.

Some people ask, "Where is there in Scripture actual ground for every believer being in the church at so-and-so?" Romans 1:7: "All the saints which are at Rome." Philippians 1:1: "All the saints who are at Philippi with the presbyters, the elders, the bishops and the deacons." In other words, it is the church—all. 1 Corinthians 1:2: "the church of God which is at Corinth, even them that are sanctified in Christ Jesus, called saints with all that call upon Him in every place." Colossians 1:2: "to the saints and faithful brethren in Christ that are at Colossae." It is inclusive. The foundation is Jesus Christ. The ground is locality. It is so simple. Once you have that, you have flung, as it were, around you all, a kind of lasso; you cannot get out.

The Local Church is Representative of Christ

The second thing is it is representative of Christ. That means it is representative of Christ in that locality. It represents Him there. It is not there to propagate peculiar or particular emphases or tenets of its own. It is simply the local church. It is simply and profoundly the body of Christ, the church of God in that city or that town or that village. That does not mean to say a church does not have an emphasis. Just as every one of us differs so all the churches differ. They are not uniform. However, there is a vast difference in having an emphasis in something because of the very way that particular company of children in that locality has gone and is existing there to propagate specifically and exclusively certain teachings or experiences or something else.

In this matter of the church being representative of Christ locally, may I say how glorious that is?! It is the most glorious calling any of us could possibly have to represent Christ in an area. How glorious that is! It means that the Lord commits Himself. He commits His authority; He commits Himself to us because it is the church, not that we are anything. That is what is so amazing! You can have an elite group of people, but the Holy Spirit will not commit Himself. But get a weak people with every kind of failing and the Lord commits Himself. Then you scratch your head and wonder what it is. It is a matter of the church because the Lord says, "I am represented here."

Will you note in this connection that in the Scripture the churches are never associated with any name or title other than that of God, "churches of God," or of Christ, or locality? Now this is very interesting. In 1 Thessalonians 1:1: "To the church of the Thessalonians." It is not the church which is at Thessalonica, but the church of the Thessalonians. In Colossians 4:16 it is: "to the church of the Laodiceans." Even more remarkably in Revelation 1:11 it says, "... write it to the seven churches, to Ephesus, Smyrna, and so on." The Lord actually calls the church by its locality, not anything else—not the Apollonian or Lutheran, Wesleyan, and all the rest of it. He says, "To Richmond, to Ashford." It is amazing!

The Local Church is Responsible Locally

Lastly, it is responsible locally. While the local church must ever remember that it is part of the whole family and seek to maintain that church consciousness, the primary responsibility of the local church is its own locality. It has within its very being, inherently within its constitution, a worldwide commission and vision and woe betide any church that loses it. Right in the very fabric of its being, at the very heart of the warp and woof out of which it is made is this worldwide vision and commission. But never think that God lets you escape from your responsibilities by serving the interest of God on the other side of the globe in an abstract way. That is the whole point again. How do we discharge first of all this worldwide vision and commission? By discharging our responsibilities locally, we are doing that. That is why the Lord said, "Ye shall be witnesses unto Me in Jerusalem, Judea, Samaria, and to the uttermost parts of the earth." We are responsible locally. It means that we as a company will one day stand before God and be held responsible for this area.

I think you see that the local church cannot be national, cannot be denominational, cannot be interdenominational, cannot be sectarian, cannot be exclusive, cannot be propagators of certain truth or aspects of it. It is simply the church of God, the body of the Lord Jesus Christ which is found at so and so. Now the vital importance of all that we have spoken about, and I believe it is, can be seen when we realise that God's purpose at Pentecost was that Christ should continue to be seen and to be expressed on earth through His body. The enemy has struck very effectively at the one and only method God has of expressing the

Lord Jesus corporately through the centuries. What a battle there has been over this thing! May the Lord help us.

Dear Lord, we commit ourselves to Thee. We pray that Thou wouldst give us that Spirit of wisdom and revelation in the knowledge of Thyself. We need it, Lord. Otherwise, all this will just be theoretical knowledge, head knowledge. Lord, in this particular subject, perhaps more than many other, Thou knowest it is so possible. We ask Thee, Lord, that we should see this thing and see it in its relationship to true spirituality, to true godliness, to overcoming, to the bride of the Lamb. We ask Thee, Lord, that Thou wouldst help us in all these things, and we ask it in the name of our Lord Jesus Christ. Amen.

2.
The Manifested Presence of Christ

Matthew 18:19–20

Again I say unto you, that if two of you shall agree on earth as touching anything that they shall ask, it shall be done for them of my Father who is in heaven. For where two or three are gathered together in my name, there am I in the midst of them.

Acts 1:1–2

The former treatise I made, O Theophilus, concerning all that Jesus began both to do and to teach, until the day in which he was received up, after that he had given commandment through the Holy Spirit unto the apostles whom he had chosen.

(I want you to note: "concerning all that Jesus began both to do and to teach.")

Ephesians 1:22–23

And he put all things in subjection under his feet,

and gave him to be head over all things to the church, which is his
body, the fullness of him that filleth all in all.

Colossians 3:10–11
And have put on the new man, that is being renewed unto knowledge
after the image of him that created him: where there cannot be Greek
and Jew, circumcision and uncircumcision, barbarian, Scythian,
bondman, freeman; but Christ is all, and in all.

II Corinthians 3:3
Being made manifest that ye are an epistle of Christ, ministered by
us, written not with ink, but with the Spirit of the living God;
not in tables of stone, but in tables that are hearts of flesh.

(Ye are a letter of Christ.)

I Corinthians 14:24–25
But if all prophesy, and there come in one unbelieving or unlearned,
he is reproved by all, he is judged by all; the secrets of his heart are
made manifest; and so he will fall down on his face and worship God,
declaring that God is among you indeed.

Revelation 1:12–13a, 20
And I turned to see the voice that spake with me. And having turned
I saw seven golden candlesticks; and in the midst of the candlesticks
one like unto a son of man ... The mystery of the seven stars which
thou sawest in my right hand, and the seven golden candlesticks or

lampstands. *The seven stars are the angels of the seven churches: and the seven candlesticks or lampstands are seven churches.*

Zechariah 4:1–10

And the angel that talked with me came again, and waked me, as a man that is wakened out of his sleep. And he said unto me, What seest thou? And I said, I have seen, and, behold, a candlestick all of gold, with its bowl upon the top of it, and its seven lamps thereon; there are seven pipes to each of the lamps, which are upon the top thereof; and two olive-trees by it, one upon the right side of the bowl, and the other upon the left side thereof. And I answered and spake to the angel that talked with me, saying, What are these, my lord? Then the angel that talked with me answered and said unto me, Knowest thou not what these are? And I said, No, my lord.

Then he answered and spake unto me, saying, This is the word of the Lord unto Zerubbabel, saying, Not by might, nor by power, but by my Spirit, saith the Lord of hosts. Who art thou, O great mountain? Before Zerubbabel thou shalt become a plain; and he shall bring forth the top stone with shoutings of Grace, grace, unto it. Moreover the word of the Lord came unto me, saying, The hands of Zerubbabel have laid the foundation of this house; his hands shall also finish it; and thou shalt know that the Lord of hosts hath sent me unto you. For who hath despised the day of small things? for these seven shall rejoice, and shall see the plummet in the hand of Zerubbabel; these are the eyes of the Lord, which run to and fro through the whole earth.

Exodus 25:31–32, 36–40

And thou shalt make a candlestick of pure gold: of beaten work shall the candlestick be made, even its base, and its shaft; its cups, its knops, and its flowers, shall be of one piece with it; and there shall be six branches going out of the sides thereof; three branches of the candlestick out of the one side thereof, and three branches of the candlestick out of the other side thereof ... Their knops and their branches shall be of one piece with it; the whole of it one beaten work of pure gold. And thou shalt make the lamps thereof, seven: and they shall light the lamps thereof, to give light over against it. And the snuffers thereof, and the snuff dishes thereof, shall be of pure gold.

Of a talent of pure gold shall it be made, with all these vessels. And see that thou make them after their pattern which hath been showed thee in the mount.

Exodus 27:20–21

And thou shalt command the children of Israel, that they bring unto thee pure olive oil beaten for the light, to cause a lamp to burn continually. In the tent of meeting, without the veil which is before the testimony, Aaron and his sons shall keep it in order from evening to morning before the Lord: it shall be a statute for ever throughout their generations on the behalf of the children of Israel.

The Church Which is His Body

Now I come to the last point that I want to make in answer to the question: Why are you at Halford House? (We have previously covered six points and this is the seventh.) For those of you who were with us some ten or eleven years ago we never covered this point then, and perhaps it was a point we did not see. My seventh point is this: The church, which is His body, is the manifested presence of Christ. I will repeat that: The church, which is His body, is the manifested presence of Christ. Having said all that we have said thus far, and we have said quite a lot, we need once more to ask ourselves one simple question: Why is the supreme figure used of the church in the New Testament the figure of the body? This figure of the body is used more than any other symbol or figure of the church. Why? We have said quite a lot in these past messages in touching upon various things which are, shall we say, more earthly in outworking, practical in content, and so on. If we were to leave it there I believe we have lost perhaps the most vital point of all in this matter of the recovery of the church.

The Body, the Expression of Personality

What is a body? It is a good question. It is nothing if it is not the means by which the personality of a person is expressed. What else is a body for? A body is the place where your personality is located. Your body is not your personality; your body is the place where your personality is located, but it is more than located. In some cases it may be only located, but generally speaking, your personality is located in a body as the means by which it expresses itself. Your personality is expressed, if you are released in some way apart from Christian things, in the way you dress, in the way you behave, in your carriage, in your reactions, in your gestures, in your stipulations. All these things express the kind of person you are; they give you away. That is why some people, especially British people, are inhibited. They are frightened to death of giving themselves away. They would prefer to keep themselves entirely private, but that fact itself gives them away. Then we discover the kind of people that are inside the body.

The body is the means by which the mind of a person, the heart of a person and the will of a person is manifested. My heart is manifested, is expressed through my body. If I have feelings, they come out through the body, if only in the eyes which are often called the windows of the soul. Or maybe your will comes out. You can see it as you get older in the lines on your face. You cannot help it. No cosmetics or foundation creams in the world will get rid of those lines which betray the will of a person. In the end, our bodies express our will through the posture that we take, in the facial expressions that so often we use. Or again, the mind is expressed through the body because in the end everything a man thinks finally determines the way he behaves. Therefore the body is supremely a means of expression. It is the means of manifesting the inward person. The invisible part of you is expressed and manifested through your body.

The Bride and the City of God

The church is the body of Christ. The church is His manifested presence. His mind, His heart and His will are to be expressed, manifested through His body. Certainly we can say, and all of us would agree that that is gloriously true of the church in the future. I think everyone agrees that one day the church is going to be the bride, the wife of the Lamb, the city in which there is no actual throne or temple. However, the Lamb is there and the glory of God shines out in a radiance, as I have often described it, rather like an electric light bulb. You can only see the shape of the bulb when the light is off, but if it is transparent and clear when the light is on you lose all shape of the bulb in the glory of the light that radiates out of that bulb. That is what the city of God will be like—it is made of gold and transparent as glass. You have never seen gold like that. From one end of the city to the other end of the city there is not one single thing that could cast a shadow. It is transparent throughout from end to end, which of course is symbolic. It is the glory of God that lightens it, and the nations walk in the light thereof.

II Thessalonians 1:10a says: "When he shall come to be glorified in his saints, and to be marvelled at in all them that believed."

I think that is a wonderful word. "Marvelled at"—people will just marvel one day. Who are those that are marvelled at? One day the glory of the Lord, the character of the Lord, the beauty of the Lord, the power of the Lord, the infinite grace and mercy of the Lord are going to be marvelled at in you and me. People are going to look at us and say, "Goodness, is that what came out of that rotten material? Is that what God could do with that unworthy, ugly substance?" Certainly the angels will marvel as they look on. I do not know what the nations are that walk in the light of it, but they are going to marvel too at what they see in the church of God.

We have it again in Revelation 21:11 in symbolic form. It is speaking of the bride, the wife of the Lamb, the holy city Jerusalem coming down out of heaven from God. It says, "Having the glory of God: her light was like unto a stone most precious, as it were a jasper stone, clear as crystal."

Verse 22–24a: "And I saw no temple therein: for the Lord God the Almighty, and the Lamb, are the temple thereof. And the city hath no need of the sun, neither of the moon, to shine upon it: for the glory of God did lighten it, and the lamp thereof is the Lamb. And the nations shall walk amidst the light thereof." Isn't that amazing!

The Church on Earth Now

I think we can all be absolutely agreed that one day it will be so glorious and wonderful that our hearts can hardly take it in. One day the church, the body of our Lord Jesus Christ, the bride, the wife of the Lamb, the holy city, new Jerusalem is going to be His manifested presence. All His excellencies, all His glory, all His character, all His beauty, all His resources will be manifested, revealed, shown, known through the church. I think we all can agree to that. But surely, and this is the point, that is as certainly true today as it is of the church in the future. What I mean is that although the full glory of all of that remains for the future, the principle holds good. We are not going to *become* the body of the Lord; we *are* the body of the Lord *now*. The principle of His manifesting His presence through His body, the church, in a practical expression in time and on earth holds good.

For instance, look at the little word in 1 Corinthians 12:27a: "Now ye are the body of Christ;" not you will be the body of Christ. You are the body of Christ right here and now. The whole point of a body is that it manifests the life that is within it. It manifests the character that is within it. It manifests the mind, the heart and the will of the person who is resident, located in that body. "Ye are the body of Christ."

Jesus Continues to Do and to Teach

That is why we read that little word in Acts 1:1. "The former treatise I made, O Theophilus, concerning all that Jesus began both to do and to teach."

We generally understand and accept that the one who wrote Acts was Dr. Luke, and he is referring to his first work which we now know is the Gospel according to Luke. It is often missed that in the early church the Gospel according to Luke and the book of Acts were together. They were two parts of one work. The Gospel according to Luke was that which Jesus began both to do and to teach. The Acts was that which Jesus continued to do and to teach. However, the Gospel according to Luke was that which the Lord Jesus began both to do and to teach personally—the Head of the new man. Acts is that which He continued both to do and to teach in and through His body. We often overlook that little word *began*, "what Jesus *began* both to do and teach." It is most interesting. For the whole inference is, the implication is that the Lord Jesus is going on doing and teaching. But how? By His Holy Spirit. But where? In and through the church.

We are now on this earth, the members of Christ. 1 Corinthians 6:15 says: "Know ye not that your bodies are members of Christ?" This word members just means "parts of a whole." You know we use the word dismember for example, to *dismember* a body. We are members of Christ; we are part of Christ. We are parts of

Him. We are like His arms, His legs, His feet, and His hands. We are His members; we belong to Him in that intimate way.

The Body, the Fullness of the Head

Again we have it in the term which we have quoted a number of times, the body, because all the members together constitute a body. In Romans 12:5 we are told: "Ye are one body in Christ." Or you could put it another way: "We are His complement, His fullness. This would almost seem blasphemous if the Scripture did not say it. But in Ephesians 1:22–23 we read of "the body which is the fullness of him who filleth all in all." He fills everything in everyone and thus the body becomes His fullness, His complement.

Every single member of my body, every single function, every single organ is filled, as it were, by my head. My head fills every single part of my body, fills everything in every one. Without my head they could not work. My head is the thing that gives them harmony and cohesion, and thus my whole body becomes the fullness, the complement of my head. In other words, my head expresses itself through my body. My body, my arms, my hands become the complement of my head. If I were to say, "Do you see the picture on the left-hand wall?" Which picture? But if I point with my finger and say, "Do you see the picture here on the left hand wall?" Immediately you know. My finger has become the complement of my head. It has been the means by which my head expresses itself—expresses its mind, expresses its will, expresses its feeling.

In precisely this way, Christ would, through us, move and think and will and love. This is the whole point of the church. It is not that we might just have meetings, or just have Bible studies, or that we might just sort of knock up against one another now and again as if that did any good in itself. That is not the point of the church. The real point of the church is that Christ may be able to think through us, act through us, move through us, love through us, will through us. That is the point of the church. Do not think it is anything other than this. The rest may be valuable and may have a part, but that is the supreme glory of union with Christ. Furthermore, it is the thing the Lord looks for as the goal, the high calling with which you and I have been called. We are not just going to sit draped around heaven, playing harps, singing little songs. The Lord has a glorious calling and vocation for the church. We do not even know what it is, except that it is in the most intimate, glorious and eternal union with Himself in such a way that He can think through us, act through us, rule through us, will through us, and love through us.

If there had been no fall, if there had been no sin, all this would have taken place. Now, God in His infinite grace has brought us back into His eternal purpose. He has given us back His original goal and objective which is to achieve this calling and vocation, but unfortunately, the fall and this parenthesis of time and sin has obscured what the Lord originally was going to do once He had brought us into that union. We do not know, but it is absolutely glorious and wonderful.

Marriage—the End or the Beginning?

I have said to you before that there are two ways of looking at marriage; either it is the end or it is the beginning. Which way are we going to look at it? Is the marriage of the wife of the Lamb with the Lamb the end, or is it the beginning? Is it the end of everything? Or is it the beginning of everything? I think it is both. It is the end of one long glorious story in history of His dealings with us which have led us finally to the actual marriage. We are only betrothed at the present; we are engaged. The Jewish engagement and the Eastern engagement were a much more definite thing than our engagement. It almost means you are wedded but not completely, the consummation has not taken place. That is just where you and I are. We are betrothed, wedded, spoken for, but there is coming a day when we are actually going to be married. Now that is the end of one long history, one long story of the Lord's ways with us; but it is the beginning of a new way. We do not know anything about it. We do not know what He is going to do through us, what He is going to use us for, what is going to be in the future. We do not know anything about those things. We have got thousands and thousands of questions piled one upon the other, and it would all be speculation because the Lord has drawn a veil over the whole thing just to stop more schools of interpretation and theology. He has kept us to this one glorious way—now. He has given us to see enough of the panorama to be lifted out of a rut, out of the dead and parochial, and out of being tied down to the littleness and pettiness of life down here.

What is the Church?

When we start to look at it like that, it is just tremendous. What is the church? The church was never meant to be a mere preaching place, a mere congregation, a mere round of meetings as such, a conference centre with glorious ministry, or a mere evangelistic agency existing to get people saved, or an exclusive club of the elite with greater knowledge and fuller measure than others, who have severed themselves from the trials and gathered themselves together. That is not the church. Nor is the church a matter of mere pattern, of mere technique, of mere New Testament order, of mere function or ministries, as glorious and tremendous as they might be, or gifts, as spiritual and useful as they might be. No, the church is the very presence of Christ manifested.

Now mind you, I am not talking against gifts or ministries or function because we have said a lot about it previously. I am not talking against many of these other things—preaching, or gatherings; for the Scriptures say, "forsake not the assembling of yourselves together." I understand all of that, but do you mean to tell me that that is all the church is? A routine of meetings, a place where messages are preached, a place where prayer is made? Is that all that the church is? Is it where hymns are sung and where people now and again get saved, and where others are dragged through various trials and difficulties? Is that all that the church is? Is that what it consists of? My goodness, I have the greatest sympathy with the man on the street, the man of the world who says, "Is that all? Is that all your gospel?" I have the greatest sympathy for many of our generation who have turned completely away from Christianity as they see it, and I am talking about evangelicals. I understand it because it seems so petty, so small, as though it has nothing to say to us. Is that all the church is? This matter of the church has much, much more to say in the matter of evangelism than the way in which ninety-nine percent of the way we Christians live. These matters we have been talking about have more to say to us of all these aspects of service, transformation, so much more than any of us have hitherto realised.

Where God is Known

What is the church? The church is nothing less than the manifested presence of Christ. What do I mean? Let me put it this way. The church is the place where men and women find God and where God finds men and women. Now, I am not talking about a building. I am not talking about an institution or an organisation. I am talking about His body. There God says, "I am known," just as the temple and the tabernacle of old symbolizes this glorious truth. God says, "If you want to know Me, come; I will meet you here. This is my dwelling place. This is My habitation. This is My home. If you wish to make an offering come within My courts, and I will meet you there." There God vouchsafed to meet with man and man could be sure that he would find God. There, as it were, man could touch God and God could touch man.

Where God is Found

What is the church? The church is where the world can see and hear and touch and handle God. In other words, the church is the continuation of what the Lord Jesus began to do. That is what we mean by the testimony of Jesus. In other words, in His day it was a personal temple, but in that temple the world could find God and God could find the world. Publicans, sinners, harlots, thieves, tax gatherers, and traitors all found God in that human temple and God found them in that human temple. It did not matter who it was—the religious, the decent, like Nicodemus or Joseph of Arimathea, whoever it was, in Christ they found God and God found them.

Where God can be Touched

Let me put it another way. They could see God; they could see the colour of His eyes; they could see the tear on His face; they could see His smile. They could hear Him. They could touch Him, and they often touched Him. They were touching God.

I have always loved the story of the little woman who touched the Lord. I cannot help being a little imaginative about that little tiny lady. I have often wondered how she got through to the Lord. She must have had a tough elbow as she pressed through that great throng of people. Peter said, "Lord, with this great crush of people, how can You say: 'Who touched Me?'" That little tiny woman with an issue of blood, must have been weak I would have thought, but she elbowed her way through. Finally, that scraggy bony arm went under someone else and touched the hem of His garment and instantly she was healed. However, my point of telling the story is not that she was healed, as glorious as that is, but because everyone was touching Him. The Lord said, "Who touched Me?" Peter said, "Lord, the whole lot is crushing around You, and You say, 'Who touched Me?'" But He said, "Someone did touch Me; I felt the virtue, the power, go out of Me." Do you understand?

They were touching God. They were actually touching God. They did not know it but they were touching God.

That is why John mysteriously writes in his first letter, chapter 1:1–3a, and very few Christians realise it: "That which was from the beginning, that which we have heard, that which we have seen with our eyes, that which we beheld and our hands handled concerning the Word of life. (and the life was manifested, and we have seen, and bear witness, and declare unto you the life, the eternal life, which was with the Father, and was manifested unto us); that which we have seen and heard declare we unto you also." In other words, John was telling us that God could be seen and heard by us.

Do you know what the Lord Jesus said about that temple of His body? He said, "Destroy this temple and in three days I will raise it up" (see John 2:19). He spoke of the temple of His body, and that is precisely what happened. Now He not only has His own personal body, but there is a spiritual temple where He continues to do and to teach.

Where the Name of the Lord Jesus Is

What is the church? Do you know that the great evangelistic mission of the church is not only to preach? It is to reveal God in its very being. This, I dare to say, is where we have lost out. We have considered that it has really been a matter of preaching and we have lost the other truth by allowing that the preaching must be the presence of the church. I do not mean just the presence of people; I mean the presence of the body of Christ.

Christ never said in Matthew 18:20: "For where two or three are gathered together into my name, there I will visit them."

He never said, "Where two or three are gathered together into my name, there I will bless them." He never said, "Where two or three are gathered together into my name, there I will use them." He never said, "Where two or three are gathered together into my name, there I will rule over them." He said, "Where two or three are gathered together into my name, there am I in the midst of them." You cannot get away from it. There am I in the midst of them; the manifested presence of Christ. There ought to be the means by which He expresses Himself. I want you to note the little preposition "in." Literally, it is "into, gathered into." It is a picture of the body again. Gathered into the midst.

The members of my body are gathered into the name of Lance Lambert. They are all in my body joined to my one head, and I have the name Lance Lambert. So they are gathered together into my name, and I am in the midst of them. Where else am I? I am not on the other side of the room. I am here in the midst of my members. They are gathered together into my body; they share my name. I am in the midst of them. This is what the Lord Jesus meant.

If you want to study this, go back to the Old Testament and see what the Lord means when He says, "You shall not offer your offerings wherever you choose, but where I choose to cause My name to dwell." Where was the place where He would cause His name to dwell? Jerusalem. Where in Jerusalem? The temple. This is a picture of this one thing we are talking about. I want you also to note the little word "for" in Matthew 18:20. You will see that it says, "For, where two or three are gathered together." Please note to what the word "for" relates. Verse 18: "Verily I say unto you, What things soever ye shall bind on earth shall be bound in heaven; and what things soever ye shall loose on earth shall be loosed in heaven ... For where two or three are gathered together into my name, there am I in the midst."

Or again in verse 19: "Again I say unto you, that if two of you shall agree on earth as touching anything that they shall ask, it shall be done for them of my Father who is in heaven. For where two or three ..." The whole point is that the Lord says, "What you do is done in heaven. You bind, it is bound in heaven. You loose, it is loosed in heaven. If you are agreed together, not just agree to agree, but you agree, as used to be said by Mr. Redpath, "You are symphonised." You are somehow or other gloriously brought into harmony. Then it will be done. Why? Because "where two or three are gathered together in My name, there am I." He will express Himself, that is the point of it. He will reveal Himself through and in His own. He will convey, not only by our words and not only by our actions even, but by our being He will convey His love, His truth, His power, His authority, His grace, His faith. We could go on and on, His salvation, His life. The whole point of the church is not that someone stands up in the pulpit and says, "Christ is life," and it just sort of hangs on the air. But rather, not only are those words said, but there is in the very being of the church the thing that ratifies it so that when men and women come in they not only hear the Word of God preached but intuitively they know it is so. It is not only the words or the actions but also the being. This is the thing that is lost. Where do we find churches like this? For the most part they are just preaching places. Even there, quite honestly, what do they preach? If we could only have the Word of God preached in all these preaching places from every pulpit, it would be one thing, but even that would not be enough.

We need the presence of the Lord; we need the manifested presence of Christ through His body.

Do not just look upon me as some extremist because you have only got to read the book of Acts to see all this in black and white. Of course you will say, "What happened when Paul stood up, or Paul and Barnabas, or Paul and Silas or some of the others? There was no church?" All right, but just see what happens when the church comes into being and these great mighty evangelists are off. Does the work fall to pieces? Oh no, they come back in a little time and they appoint elders in every church. In other words, all those little groups had all blossomed and flourished, fruited and increased so that they could appoint elders in them. Isn't that extraordinary! There were no theological courses, no theological seminaries, no missionary schools, not even a Bible college. I am not saying these things have not got value. What I am saying is they seem to have done awfully well without them. Really! Now why? I suggest that it is because it is not only words and actions, but being. In other words, there was a corporate being as well as the proclamation and an executive action.

A Wife, Not Spiritual Machinery

The church therefore is not some spiritual machine or a spiritual or powerful technique, something cold, hard, correct and inanimate. The church is something which lives, and breathes, laughs and cries, travails and understands. I want to suggest to you very simply that when that is missing everything is missing. *Everything is missing*! It is as simple as that. If the church is not a breathing, living, feeling, loving thing, you can pack it up; it is over. It is just as simple as that because the church never was and never will be spiritual machinery. That is why the Lord at the end of the Bible says, "It is a wife I want, not a bit of machinery." I do not want just a spiritual technique; I do not want just a bit of spiritual machinery. I want something that lives and breathes, moves, feels, laughs, cries, travails and understands.

I suggest to you that is why the Lord is so seemingly harsh in some of His judgments. When everything seems so good, and so right, and so correct, we cannot understand why the Lord seems to be harsh in His judgment, but the Lord has always wanted a bride. If He had wanted a bit of machinery we need not have had all this mess or all this trouble. We could have done away with all the millennia of time. It would have been so utterly simple. The Lord could have gotten His machinery so perfectly, but the Lord is not interested in machinery, and it seems to me we have an earth-bound tendency in all of us to degenerate, to deteriorate to machinery. It is so much easier, isn't it? Yet it isn't easy because as soon as we degenerate to that, we know intuitively that we are not what we are supposed to be. Deep down within us there is a huge question mark. That is why you find so much unhappiness among the children of God even where you get good preaching. It is not just the old nature; of course there is the old nature and plenty of it. But it is not just the old nature; it is this deep-seated intuitive sense that we were never meant to be machinery. We were never meant to be some technique, some pattern; we were meant to be in a relationship together with Him and with one another. In other words, what I am simply saying is that the church is the new man.

I do believe that because of the way we theologically understand that phrase "the new man" we have missed the point.

The One New Man

The Lord says in Colossians 3:10–11: "And have put on the new man, wherein Christ is everything in every one."

We have the same thought in Galatians 3:28: "There can be neither Jew nor Greek, there can be neither bond nor free, there can be no male and female; for ye all are one man in Christ Jesus."

It is one new man. Now a man is a head and a body. You will see that this new man is a corporate being because in him there is neither male nor female, Jew nor Greek, bond nor free. In other words, there are many in Him. It is a corporate entity, a corporate being. This new man is head and body, Christ and His own.

Why do I say that I think many of us have missed the point in this? I do believe that we tend to think of it merely as a kind of teaching of holiness, a teaching of sanctification—you put on the new man. We miss the real point which is simply this: the church cannot be less human than her head and she cannot be more spiritual than her Head. We are the new man. He, that is the Lord Jesus, is the perfect example of the kind of humanity God wants and we share. That is how we put it on. We share a new humanity. We share a new kind of man, but the accent is on humanity. This message needs to get into Christian circles, and I am not now talking about where there is so much superficiality but rather where there is so much depth, because we have missed the point in this thing. We have become like spiritual automatons, like spiritual machines, whereas the Lord wants us to be the new man, the new humanity.

1 John 2:6: "He that saith he abideth in him ought himself also to walk even as he walked." Why did I say the church cannot be less human than the Lord? It is because many of us Christians are far less human. Jesus was never a machine. He hungered, He thirsted, He slept, He grew weary, He cried. Now some people think it is quite unspiritual to cry, and in that, they are less human than their Lord. Isn't that an extraordinary thing? Do you think God wants spiritual machinery? No. He wants something, not according to the old man, but according to the new man, and that perfect example of the new man we see in the Lord Jesus Christ.

Now when I say we are not to be more spiritual than Him, I did not mean that you could be too spiritual. But what I do mean is that kind of pseudo spirituality which is artificial and which is always machinery; it is technique. It does not come from the life within. It is not the product of the Holy Spirit; it is not the fruit of the Spirit. In my little experience every person I have really found to be full of the Lord, in whom I see the fruit of the Spirit has been so normal they could laugh and they could cry. By the way, we are not all meant to be going around weeping. Some people just do not cry. That is all right, but some people do cry—all right. We do not want that dreadful hankering after melancholia that affects some believers as if that is godliness. It is not godliness at all. But if you and I are this way or that way, then we have to be. God wants us to be human beings. Let me say it again, He does not want machinery but a bride, human beings. It is very simple when you see it like that.

In Luke 19:41 it says, "And when he drew nigh, he saw the city and wept over it." And I think I am right in saying that the word is: "He wailed." Then in John 11:35, which is the shortest verse in the Bible, it says: "Jesus wept."

I suggest to you that that one little window into the character and life of the Lord Jesus Christ reveals His absolute humanity. We know the fact He wept at Lazarus' grave has been a great point, not of controversy, but of perplexity. Why did He weep when He knew that He was going to raise him from the dead? People have come to the most marvellous and complex solutions for this because somehow they feel that it must be a bit of spiritual machinery, but He was human. He was overcome by the circumstances. He knew exactly what He was going to do, but it did not stop Him from crying.

Divine Love

We can see what I have been saying in the extraordinary way in which love has been emphasized in 1 Corinthians 13. Right in the middle of dealing with practical matters of the local church—ladies taking part, the Lord's table, gifts, their functions, harmony in the body, the priesthood of all believers, and later on the freedom of the Spirit in gatherings—and right in the middle of it, not after it, we have this most extraordinary emphasis on love. Now if it had been chapter 14 and chapter 14 had been chapter 13 we could all have understood. We would have had a wonderful treatise on love and then gone on to a wonderful treatise on resurrection. But why does this whole matter of love come right in the middle of talking about all these practical things of the church?

Here is what 1 Corinthians 12:31b says in some of the different versions:

American Standard Version
Moreover a most excellent way I show unto you.

Authorised Version
And I show unto you a more excellent way.

The Living Bible
Something else that is better than any of them.

The Twentieth Century
Yet I can still show you a way beyond all comparison the best.

Moffat
And yet I will go on to show you a still higher path.

Phillips
But I will show you a way which surpasses them all.

Look at 1 Corinthians 14:1:

Authorised Version
Follow after charity.

Williams
Keep on pursuing love.

Moffat

Make love your aim.

Monmouth

Hotly pursue this love.

Amplified

Make love your great quest.

Don't you think this is extraordinary that this comes right here? What does it mean? Isn't it exactly what I am talking about? The apostle Paul, in explaining all these practical matters of the church that have to do with order, pattern, gifts, functions and all these other very important principles, suddenly stops and says, "Now look here, lest you miss the whole point I will show you the most excellent way of all." It is not order, although that is important. It is not function; you have to have it. It is not gifts; you cannot do without them. It is not the freedom of the Spirit or the harmony of the body or the priesthood of all believers. These are all vital things, but the most important, the most excellent way of all for the Lord to get what He wants is divine love.

What is he saying? This is how most of us have understood it: "I must personally know something of love; you must personally know something of love." That is right, but really what he was trying to say was this: the church has got to become the embodiment of divine love. It has got to become the expression of divine love, not sentimental, not sloshy, not sort of all over the place, but divine love. It has got to be the kind of love that we know in God—

fervent, true, faithful, unflinching, disciplining when we need it—that kind of love. The church has got to be that—the embodiment of divine love, not the love that goes head over heels and loses itself, but the love that is patient, endures and never fails. Divine love.

That is why John, who was the nearest to our Lord, when he came to write his letter spent over three of the chapters, out of the five talking about love. It is not the love of God and that is the strange thing in one sense. If you read chapters 2, 3, 4 of 1 John you will find all he's talking about is: "If you do not love your brother, you do not love God." How do you know you love God? By your love for one another. Why was John always going on and on about this? People say, "John was so simple." Yes he was, but profound. What he was really saying was this: "If you do not know what divine love is you have lost everything. Make no mistake about it. I think it was brother Watchman Nee who said that John's great ministry was recovery. Is it not interesting that he talks so much about divine love? Just in case we get the idea that it is pattern, technique, gifts, and order. You cannot get away from it.

Leaving First Love

Perhaps the harshest word of all is in Revelation 2:4–5 where the Lord says: "But I have this against thee, that thou didst leave thy first love." He speaks to a company which he commends for their work, their labour, their faith, their toil, and then He says, "I have this against thee, thou didst leave thy first love." Then He goes on and says, "Remember therefore whence thou art fallen, and repent and do the first works." But they are still doing all the works.

The works are there. "I know thy works, and thy toil and patience." What is the difference? The first works sprang out of love.

Then He says, "Repent and do the first works or else I will come to thee and remove your lampstand." Isn't that a harsh thing to do? Couldn't we say, "Oh, but Lord, this company is on church ground? But Lord, this company has got all the principles operating. It has the freedom of the Spirit. They judge those who call themselves apostles and are not. They hate the Nicolaitans with their distinction between the clergy and the laity, and all the rest of it." But the Lord's whole point was this: if they have lost this love, they have lost it all. It is a matter of time before the whole thing goes. The bell is tolling; they are on their way to their burial, and they do not know it. They go to all the meetings, having the prayer meetings, the Bible studies, out in the streets getting people in, and all the rest of it, but they do not know they are being taken to their own funeral because they have left their first love. Now, I say that is a very harsh word if you look at it from one point of view. Why should the Lord go to such a length as that when everything else was right? I tell you why; because it is this very point I am trying to make that the church is the manifested presence of Christ.

It is this very manifestation of what God in Christ is—love, light, life—that makes the impact upon this world so that when they come in, they touch love—not a silly thing—but they know it intuitively. When someone says, "We love you," they know it. They touch light, and they know it. They touch life of another kind, and they know it. I suggest that that is what makes the impact upon this world.

Was there any New Testament locality that did not feel the impact and influence of the church there, in its beginnings? It turned the world upside down. I say it was not just a matter of preaching or merely a matter of gifts or knowledge or method. It was the manifestation of the presence of Christ, the sovereign presence of God through everything and everyone. That is why it says in 1 Corinthians 14 that the unsaved man will come in and fall on his face and say, "God is among you"—not "marvellous preaching has found me out," but God is among you, the manifested presence of God in Christ.

Manifesting Things to the Unseen World

The church is also being used to manifest things to the unseen world, let alone the seen world. It speaks of angels desiring to look into these things. Do you know that there are angels all around, hosts of them, and you and I are the object lesson to the intent that now unto the principalities and powers in the heavenly places might be made known through the church the manifold wisdom of God? It is not only for them, but the angels desire to look into these things. They are educated by what they see happening in us as the church. Do you know that every time we celebrate the Lord's table we declare His death until He comes? We do not just go through a little ceremony; we actually proclaim something in the unseen.

The apostle Paul said, "We wrestle not against flesh and blood but against principalities, against powers, against world rulers of this present darkness, against hosts of wicked spirits in the heavenlies" (see Ephesians 6:12a). Here they all are; they are being instructed. How are they being instructed? They are being made the footstool of His feet by the church. I will not say by the church but through the church because He is Head over all things to the church and every time a battle is won something more becomes the footstool of His feet. Do not think a battle is won just by always seeming to be on top. The Lord won His greatest battle when He cried out: "My God, My God, why hast Thou forsaken Me?" That is when He won the battle. That is sometimes when the church wins the battle too.

What is the Lampstand?

I read a few verses about the lampstand. We know that the lampstand speaks of the church. In Zechariah 4 it is immediately connected with the building, the top stone. In Revelation 1:20 we are told the seven golden lampstands are the seven churches. We all know that, but if you look in Exodus 25, you will see just this golden lampstand. What is it? Is it a thing of costly and valuable beauty only, an ornament? True, it is of pure gold; true, it is beaten out of one piece of gold; true, it has pure olive oil as fuel for light within its lamps. But tell me, is it just an ornament? Is it a costly ornament wrought at great cost out of pure gold with pure beaten olive oil within its lamps? We know all these things have significance. The gold speaks of the divine character and life of Christ out of which the church is formed. The beaten work of one piece speaks of His oneness. We know that, and that we are perfected into one and knit together, fitly framed. We know that. The oil speaks of the pure life of Christ by the Holy Spirit in us. But tell me, what is the point of this golden lampstand? Is it an ornament? It is of pure gold, beaten work, with oil in the lamp. If it is not a light, it is an ornament. Now that is the whole point; the church is the manifested presence of Christ. She is a light. She is on fire, if you like. There is a fire there. There is a light there. Do you understand? What I am trying to say is that the church holds the testimony of Jesus, and that light was to be a light continually from generation to generation, forever. The church is to hold the testimony of Jesus consistently and continually. It is the manifested presence of Christ.

You will find it everywhere in the book of Acts. When Ananias and Sapphira came up against it, they lost their lives. The church discovered things all over the place, within and without, of the manifested presence of Christ.

This is a hard message. It is much easier to keep to technique, the pattern, or even gifts, or function, or definition of the definition of principles, but this that I have spoken about in the ultimate and final analysis is what matters. If that is missing, I dare to say the lampstand has gone. So simple, but so true.

Shall we pray:

Now Lord, we commit ourselves to Thee. Oh Lord, this matter finds us all out, it really does, but Lord, we praise and worship Thee for Thy grace toward us all and for the shedding abroad in our hearts of that love of Thine. Now Lord, we pray that Thou wouldst keep us in that relationship with Thyself and with one another in love, in life, and in light which means that Thou can manifest Thy presence in and through us as Thy body. Oh Lord, do that we pray, and burn it into our hearts that when this matter of our relationship with Thee breaks down, the rest breaks down and when our relationship with one another breaks down, the rest breaks down. Lord, help us to hold fast the Head and find the body, and we ask it all in the name of our Lord Jesus Christ. Amen.

3.
The Testimony of Jesus

Revelation 4:1–5:14

After these things I saw, and behold, a door opened in heaven, and the first voice that I heard, a voice as of a trumpet speaking with me, one saying, Come up hither, and I will show thee the things which must come to pass hereafter. Straightway I was in the Spirit: and behold, there was a throne set in heaven, and one sitting upon the throne; and he that sat was to look upon like a jasper stone and a sardius: and there was a rainbow round about the throne, like an emerald to look upon. And round about the throne were four and twenty thrones: and upon the thrones I saw four and twenty elders sitting, arrayed in white garments; and on their heads crowns of gold. And out of the throne proceed lightnings and voices and thunders. And there were seven lamps of fire burning before the throne, which are the seven Spirits of God; and before the throne, as it were a sea of glass like unto crystal; and in the midst of the

---

throne, and round about the throne, four living creatures full of eyes before and behind. And the first creature was like a lion, and the second creature like a calf, and the third creature had a face as of a man, and the fourth creature was like a flying eagle. And the four living creatures, having each one of them six wings, are full of eyes round about and within: and they have no rest day and night, saying,

Holy, holy, holy, is the Lord God, the Almighty, who was and who is and who is to come. And when the living creatures shall give glory and honor and thanks to him that sitteth on the throne, to him that liveth for ever and ever, the four and twenty elders shall fall down before him that sitteth on the throne, and shall worship him that liveth for ever and ever, and shall cast their crowns before the throne, saying,

Worthy art thou, our Lord and our God, to receive the glory and the honor and the power: for thou didst create all things, and because of thy will they were, and were created.

And I saw in the right hand of him that sat on the throne a book written within and on the back, close sealed with seven seals. And I saw a strong angel proclaiming with a great voice, Who is worthy to open the book, and to loose the seals thereof? And no one in the heaven, or on the earth or under the earth, was able to open the book, or to look thereon. And I wept much, because no one was found worthy to open the book, or to look thereon: and one of the elders saith unto me, Weep not; behold, the Lion that is of the tribe of Judah, the Root of David, hath overcome to open the book and the seven seals thereof. And I saw in the mist of the throne and of the four living creatures, and in the midst of the elders, a Lamb standing, as though it had been slain, having seven horns, and seven eyes, which are the seven Spirits of God, sent forth into all the earth. And he came, and he taketh it out of the right hand of him that sat on the throne. And when he had taken the book, the four living creatures and the four and twenty elders fell down before the Lamb, having each one a harp, and golden bowls full of incense, which are the prayers of the saints. And they sing a new song, saying,

Worthy art thou to take the book, and to open the seals thereof: for thou wast slain, and didst purchase unto God with thy blood men of every tribe, and tongue, and people, and nation, and madest them to be unto our God a kingdom and priests; and they reign upon the earth.

And I saw, and I heard a voice of many angels round about the throne and the living creatures and the elders; and the number of them was ten thousand times ten thousand, and thousands of thousands; saying with a great voice,

Worthy is the Lamb that hath been slain to receive the power, and riches, and wisdom, and might, and honor, and glory, and blessing.

And every created thing which is in the heaven, and on the earth, and under the earth, and on the sea, and all things that are in them, heard I saying,

Unto him that sitteth on the throne, and unto the Lamb, be the blessing, and the honor, and the glory, and the dominion, for ever and ever.

And the four living creatures said, Amen. And the elders fell down and worshipped.

I want to go straight to the next point which I feel we ought to make, one of which I am quite sure there is much need of instruction. It is all summed up in this phrase: *the testimony of Jesus*. I think the Lord has spoken to us in the past year or two a number of times about the testimony of Jesus and about the golden lampstand. I am also quite sure that many of us use the phrase *the testimony of Jesus,* if we use it at all, without really understanding its significance. It is a kind of phrase that once you get hold of it you can use it without really understanding exactly what it means. It is this subject that I want to deal with by the grace of God. Everything depends upon the illumination the Holy Spirit can give to us as we turn to His Word.

This phrase is used mostly in the book of Revelation. Elsewhere it is only used a few times in the New Testament. Unfortunately, in your modern, colloquial versions the phrase has been completely obliterated and is rendered as "giving testimony to Jesus" or "witnessing to Jesus." This is rather sad, and I do not quite understand why this has been interpreted in this way since it is a very simple genitive. It is the testimony of Jesus.

Testimony–Witness–Martyr

The word *testimony* in the New Testament is the word also rendered "witness," and in Greek there is no other word for *martyr*. Our English word martyr is the word "witness." It comes from the same word for *testimony*. A witness is a martyr; it is the same thing. You have to understand by the context whether it is a witness who has lost his life for his testimony. There is no difference in the word.

In spite of the fact that our modern, colloquial versions have obscured the meaning of this phrase, it is a phrase, in my estimation, of very great importance and significance indeed.

Biblical References to the Testimony of Jesus

Let's look at all the references we have in the Bible to the testimony of Jesus.

John, who bare witness of the word of God, and of the testimony of Jesus Christ, even of all things that he [John] saw.
Revelation 1:2

I John, your brother and partaker with you in the tribulation and kingdom and patience which are in Jesus, was in the isle that is called Patmos, for the word of God and the testimony of Jesus.
Revelation 1:9

And the dragon waxed wroth with the woman, and went away to make war with the rest of her seed, that keep the commandments of God, and hold the testimony of Jesus.
Revelation 12:17

And I fell down before his feet to worship him. And he saith unto me, See thou do it not: I am a fellow-servant with thee and with thy brethren that hold the testimony of Jesus: worship God: for the testimony of Jesus is the spirit of prophecy.
Revelation 19:10

*I thank my God always concerning you, for the grace of God
which was given you in Christ Jesus; that in everything ye were
enriched in him, in all utterance and all knowledge; even as
the testimony of Christ was confirmed in you: so that ye come
behind in no gift; waiting for the revelation of our Lord
Jesus Christ.*
1 Corinthians 1:4–7

*And I, brethren, when I came unto you, came not with
excellency of speech or of wisdom, proclaiming to you the
testimony of God.*
1 Corinthians 2:1

In the English Revised Version this is rendered "mystery of God,"
but in the Authorised Version, the American Standard Version,
and the Revised Standard Version it is rendered "Testimony of
God." Compare that with what has gone before.

*Be not ashamed therefore of the testimony of our Lord, nor of
me his prisoner; but suffer hardship with the gospel according to
the power of God.*
II Timothy 1:8

(Be not ashamed therefore of the testimony of our Lord.)

And from Jesus Christ, who is the faithful witness.
Revelation 1:5

It is very easy to just read this kind of thing again and again as a Christian and never think of what it means. What does it mean "the faithful witness"? The word witness again is just the same word as "martyr," or "testifier" if you will.

These things saith the Amen, the faithful and true witness.
Revelation 3:14b

It seems to me reasonably clear from these passages that this phrase the testimony of Jesus does not refer merely to some general and ordinary witnessing on our part to the Lord Jesus Christ, but to something far greater and of much deeper significance. I believe it refers to that testimony which the Lord Jesus Himself bore and indeed expressed in Himself in His very being.

God's True Nature and Character

The testimony of Jesus was to God's true character. In all the falsity of ideas about God—about the nature of God and the existence of God—He bore testimony to the true nature of God's character. He bore testimony to God's will and to God's purpose from eternity to eternity in a world which had lost in every way any idea of the aim or the objective for which it was created. He bore testimony to God's eternal and original purpose for man and for the whole creation. He bore testimony to God's ways, to God's heart, to God's redeeming love and salvation by which He could and would restore and reconcile a fallen humanity which was degraded, perverted, corrupted, and alienated. He bore testimony to the way that God could restore and reconcile that fallen humanity to His original glorious destiny.

The Foundation of the World System

It is into this world that is blind, disobedient and sinful, which has long since forfeited the right to God's mercy and forgiveness that the Lord Jesus came. He came into a world, mark you, that is founded upon a lie. We must get rid of all our sentimental ideas about this world—its beautiful sunsets, its twittering birds, the magnificence of things all around us. They are all there. There is no doubt about that, but the fact is that this whole system of things into which you and I have been born is founded and built on a lie. Instead of finding its centre, its meaning, its very existence and life in God, it now finds its life and existence in selfhood. This has crept into every sphere and every part of the creation. It is a world founded and built on a lie, and this lie has poisoned the very life-blood of humanity. *It is in us.*

My dear child of God, whoever you are, however long you have been in the way, the nearer you get to God the more you find this lie which is in our blood stream. Think of it. The moment the Lord takes action with us, what is our first reaction? Is it to fall flat on our faces and worship Him? —never! Our first reaction is: "Why did You do that to me?" We distrust God; we always believe the worst about God. We rebel against God; we react against Him. Why do we do this? It is our spontaneous reaction. Our spontaneous reaction is not always to believe the best about God, to believe that He is doing it for our best, that He is leading in the best way, or that He can undertake for us. Otherwise, I dare to say that as many issues as there are believers, including myself, would be settled right now. Behind all this holding on to ourselves, all this refusal to let go, lies this poisoned bloodstream, this life-blood that has been poisoned, which is in us all. We do not trust God. We believe He is a grabber, a grasper, someone who wants to dictate to us, someone who does not really want our joy and our wellbeing, but in fact actually wants to make us miserable, empty and negative if it is at all possible. Some perhaps are not so deeply poisoned as others. But I am quite sure that when we begin to discover the work of the Holy Spirit in our lives, this is one of the things that soon becomes very apparent to us all. Our very life-blood has been poisoned by a lie.

Inverted Values

The values of this world have been inverted. As Christians, part of our life-long education by the Holy Spirit is to bring us to true values, to see things that are real values as against what we have thought to be values. This world's values are inverted values. It is a world in which its meaningfulness has been lost. When you think of this world, when you go to work in the morning and you look around the bus, or when you get to the office, or wherever it is that you go, you see people rushing here, rushing there, going through life, through a routine of activity, all to drop dead at the end. Some not bothering to ask where they came from or where they are going, caught up in a great machinery called life, its meaningfulness lost. What is the point of it all in the end?

Of course, if you accept these false values then you can be slightly happier sometimes till death comes or illness comes or something else comes and then suddenly you are face to face with reality. It is a world that is lost to God, lost to eternal life and lost to the glory of God. It is a world that has been relegated to the iron-like bondage of sin and death, a prison house of darkness and blindness.

That is the world you and I know, a world whose vicious principle is self-centredness, a world which is inflated by pride, a world which is alienated from the life of God. It is into this world that the Lord Jesus came. He came bearing testimony to the genuine reality of all things, bearing testimony to the true character of it all.

I am not just talking about God, but the Lord Jesus by His very presence suddenly made men and women realise they were not meant for this. Suddenly prostitutes, publicans, sinners began to wake up to the fact that this was not life, that they were lost, that there was something more than just an idea. There was a possibility of something. He awakened something in people. It is the testimony that He bore. It was His very presence as well as His preaching that brought another world to bear upon people, another kingdom to bear upon people, another life to bear upon people. It was not merely that He interpreted and defined for us something about God, about His true nature, about His character. It is not just that He revealed, proclaimed and declared God, but that He showed us what we were made of. He showed us the dark side of the coin as well as the bright side. In the Bible you will find it in many, many places:

He that cometh from above is above all: he that is of the earth is
of the earth, and of the earth he speaketh: he that cometh from
heaven is above all. What he hath seen and heard, of that he
beareth testimony and no man receiveth his testimony. He that
hath receiveth his testimony hath set his seal to this, that God
is true [real]. For he whom God hath sent speaketh the words
of God: for he giveth not the Spirit by measure. The Father
loveth the Son, and hath given all things into his hand. He that
believeth on the Son hath eternal life; but he that obeyeth not
the Son shall not see life, but the wrath of God abideth on him.
John 3:31–36

I can of myself do nothing: as I hear, I judge: and my judgment
is righteous; because I seek not mine own will, but the will of
him that sent me. If I bear testimony of myself, my testimony is
not true. It is another that beareth testimony of me; and I know
that the testimony which he testified of me is true. Ye have
sent unto John, and he hath borne testimony unto the truth.
But the testimony which I receive is not from man: howbeit I
say these things, that ye may be saved. He was the lamp that
burneth and shineth; and ye were willing to rejoice for a season
in his light. But the testimony which I have is greater than
that of John; for the works which the Father hath given me to
accomplish, the very works that I do, bear witness of me,
that the Father hath sent me. And the Father that sent me,
he hath borne testimony of me. Ye have neither heard his voice
at any time, nor seen his form.
John 5:30–37

Again therefore Jesus spake unto them, saying, I am the light of
the world: he that followeth me shall not walk in the darkness,
but shall have the light of life. The Pharisees therefore said
unto him, Thou bearest testimony of thyself; thy testimony is
not true. Jesus answered and said unto them, Even if I bear
testimony of myself, my testimony is true; for I know whence I
came, and whither I go; but ye know not whence I come,
or whither I go. Ye judge after the flesh; I judge no man. Yea and
if I judge, my judgment is true; for I am not alone, but I and the
Father that sent me. Yea and in your law it is written, that the
witness of two men is true. I am he that beareth testimony of
myself, and the Father that sent me beareth testimony of me.
John 8:12–18

Pilate therefore said unto him, Art thou a king then?
Jesus answered, Thou sayest that I am a king. To this end have
I been born, and to this end am I come into the world, that I
should bear testimony unto the truth.
John 18:37a

Turn back to John 3. There are a few verses more which I would
like to read which act as a commentary on these others.

And this is the judgment, that the light is come into the world,
and men loved the darkness rather than the light; for their
works were evil. For every one that doeth evil hateth the light,
and cometh not to the light, lest his works should be reproved.
But he that doeth the truth cometh to the light, that his works

may be made manifest, that they have been wrought in God.
John 3:19–21

Two Essential Revelations

The testimony of Jesus is much more than merely a testimony by lip or words. It is much more than the truth He proclaimed. He not only bore testimony, He was that testimony Himself. It was not only on His lips but in His very being. He was Himself the very expression of what God was like and what God wanted, the kind of Person God is and the kind of man God wants. The moment we look at the Lord Jesus, we see two things together—inextricably together and yet quite distinct. We see in the Lord Jesus the kind of Person God is, the heart of God revealed, the mind of God revealed, and we see in the Lord Jesus the kind of man that you and I should be. Immediately we see the kind of Person God is and we see the kind of person God originally intended for you and me to be. That is the testimony.

We have that again in all kinds of scriptures:

No man has seen God at any time; the only begotten Son,
who is in the bosom of the Father, he hath declared him.
John 1:18

The Word became flesh, and dwelt among us (and we beheld
his glory, glory as of the only begotten from the Father), full of
grace and truth.
John 1:14

It was not just what He preached; it was that in Him, in His very being was the testimony. He was full of grace and truth. We beheld the glory as of the only begotten of the Father.

Jesus saith unto him ... He that hath seen me hath seen the
Father.
John 14:9

He said, "He that hath seen me hath seen him that sent me."
John 12:45

Hath at the end of these days spoken unto us in his Son, whom
he appointed heir of all things, through whom also he made
the worlds; who being the effulgence of his glory, and the very
image of his substance ...
Hebrews 1:2–3a

It is beyond us, isn't it? That is the kind of Person God is. He is revealed in the Lord Jesus. How can any finite created being understand God? We cannot. God is Spirit. God is infinite. God is vast. God is holy and incomprehensibly beyond us. No little created intelligence can ever fathom God, can ever even understand God; but in the Lord Jesus Christ God has a human form. Suddenly God becomes focused. God becomes understandable (if you see what I mean). He has a colour to His eyes, a colour to His hair, an actual shape to His face, hands that worked at a carpenter's bench. There were lines on His face that portrayed the years of labour that He went through, and so on. He could weep, He could hunger, and He could thirst. In all these things we see the kind of Person God is; but we also see the kind of person God wants.

If we read those terrifying chapters, Matthew 5, 6, 7, which we normally call the Sermon on the Mount, and start to measure ourselves by them, every one of us comes short. There is only one Person of whom that Sermon on the Mount is a perfect example and that is the Lord Jesus. In every single part of it He perfectly and absolutely expressed the kind of man God intended us to be originally. No wonder the apostle Peter in writing a letter later on said: "Christ left us an example that we should follow" (see 1 Peter 2:21). That is what we call the testimony of Jesus. But I want to take it further.

The Eight Signs in John's Gospel

It is even more clearly seen in the eight great claims that the Lord Jesus made and upon which John based his gospel—those eight tremendous claims: I AM. It is not without significance that the one who saw the visions in the book of Revelation and who uses this phrase, *the testimony of Jesus,* more than anyone else, is the one who in his gospel gathers everything around these eight great claims of the Lord Jesus Christ.

I AM the bread of life.
John 6:48

I AM the light of world: he that followeth Me shall not walk in the darkness, but shall have the light of life.
John 8:12a

Before Abraham was born, I AM.
John 8:58

(It is the whole explanation of Jewish history.)

I AM the door.
John 10:9a

I AM the good Shepherd.
John 10:11a

I AM the resurrection, and the life: he that believeth on me,
though he die, yet shall he live; and whosoever liveth and
believeth on me shall never die.
John 11: 25

I AM the way, and the truth, and the life: no one cometh unto
the Father, but by me.
John 14:6

I AM the true vine.
John 15:1a

This is the last one and surely the top stone.

John sets down these eight great claims one by one, not haphazardly in his gospel, but with a great design into which he weaves eight great signs. I am not going to go through the signs because that is not so important for our current study. He weaves eight great signs and a number of other incidents and through the whole thing John tries to set before us the testimony of Jesus.

Jesus did not say, "I give the bread of life, or I produced the bread of life." He said, "I AM the bread of life." Jesus did not say, "I AM the culmination of the history of the Old Testament." He said, "I AM the history of the Old Testament, before Abraham was I AM." He did not say, "I point to the door." He said, "I AM the door." He did not say, "I give the life." He said, "I AM the resurrection and the life" not merely that He will raise us one day but He is the resurrection and the life. It is not just what He preaches, but what He is in Himself. This is the testimony of Jesus.

Turning the Water into Wine

I would like to give you a few samples of what the testimony of Jesus means in practice from this gospel of John. In chapter 2, the very first sign is the turning of water into wine. I have often thought there are many, many Christians who should have a great problem with this. After all, if the Lord had followed the right thing He should have turned the wine into water. But He turned water into wine and just so no one can get away from it, it was the very best vintage wine. Those who knew quite a lot about wine said, "You have kept the best to the last, the really good old vintage you brought out at the end."

What was the Lord Jesus doing? Of course, this is no excuse at all for us to go on the bottle. The whole point that the Lord Jesus was making was this: It was corruptible into incorruptible. It is the testimony of Jesus. In the East water is the most dangerous thing in this world. Leave it in a stone jar for more than a day or two and it stagnates and a whole village can be wiped out with cholera. It was corruptible. You can leave wine for year after year and the higher the percentage of alcohol the safer it is. It is incorruptible.

It says expressly in chapter 2:11: "This beginning of His signs did Jesus ..." not miracles, but signs. A sign is more than a miracle. It is a miracle with significance. "This beginning of his signs did Jesus in Cana of Galilee, and manifested his glory." Glory! Who can change corruptible into incorruptible? Oh, my poor old body. I am not so old but I have an old corruptible body, and it is getting older all the time. You also have a corruptible body, but one day the Lord Jesus—Oh, the glory of it!—is going to turn it into something incorruptible.

The Lord Jesus in the Temple

Again, in the last part of chapter 2 you will see what I mean about this testimony of Jesus. The Lord Jesus went into the temple and did something which has upset some people. Seemingly He lost His temper. In the white fury of His anger He deliberately made a scourge of knots and turned over all the tables and caused pandemonium in the outer court of the temple. He said, "You shall not make My Father's house a house of commerce." Would to God that many of us Christians could hear the Word of the Lord in this matter. "You shall not make My Father's house a house of commerce, merchandise." Then He said, "Destroy this temple and in three days I will raise it up" (v. 19)—the testimony of Jesus. "This that you see in all these bricks is nothing," says the Lord Jesus. "This is the temple. Destroy it and in three days I will raise it up an incorruptible eternal temple, a habitation of God in the Spirit in which all nations shall find their house of prayer—the testimony of Jesus.

The Discussion with Nicodemus

In chapter 3 there is another incident. One of the greatest Bible teachers in Israel came to the Lord Jesus by night to discuss things with Him about His claims and the basis of His miracles and signs. The Lord Jesus brushed the whole lot aside and said, "Verily, verily, I say unto you, Except a man be born anew, born from above, born again, he cannot see the kingdom of heaven" (see v. 3). Then He goes on: "You must be born of water, born of the Spirit. That which is born of the flesh is flesh; that which is born of the Spirit is spirit" (see vv. 4–6). Here is the testimony of Jesus.

The Lord Jesus came into a situation which was cultured, educated, religious, pious, and decent. Suddenly the light of God shone into that darkened and alienated heart even though it was decent, upright, moral, and pious. Dear old Nicodemus must have spun like a top. Then he says, "What do you mean? Born again? Must I enter my mother's womb?" (v. 4). Of course not. That was a very silly thing to say. In the end Nicodemus was converted and understood it all. But do you see where that light first shone in? It shone into a cultured, religious, educated pious man who thought he was doing everything that was required of him? Suddenly it was the testimony of Jesus.

"That which is of the earth is earthy" (see 3:31). That is what it says here in explanation of this very thing. Poor Nicodemus. In the end he says, "How can these things be?" "Ah," says the

Lord Jesus, "it cannot be by human ingenuity or creativeness or cleverness. It will come just as the serpent was lifted up by Moses in the wilderness. Even so must the Son of Man be lifted up (v. 14). That which has poisoned mankind, which has poisoned and destroyed even the best and the most decent of mankind I am going to take into Myself on the cross and die for. Then the way will be opened up for the Spirit of God to come into your heart when you are washed and cleansed from your sin and enter into a new birth. Then you are no longer born of the earth earthy but born of heaven, born from above." It is just marvellous when you see it.

The Woman at the Well

In the next chapter, chapter 4, there is the woman of Samaria. She bounced along to the well with her pot on her head to fetch her water. I have no doubt that she had sorrows and troubles and trials in her life. Most of those ladies had. (You cannot marry five husbands without some sorrow, I should think.) Jauntily she goes along to the well and the Lord Jesus says to her, "Could I have a cup of water?" That was the first thing—the testimony of Jesus. Our idea of the testimony of Jesus is quite different. We would have thought He would have stood there and pierced her through with a holy look so that she shrivelled and all her five husbands flitted before her eyes. But no, not at all!

The Lord Jesus said to her in a quite spontaneous way: "Could I have a cup of water?" "Why," she said, "Sir, aren't you a Jew?" "Yes, I am." Then she said, "But Sir, Jews have no dealings with Samaritans."

She did not say who she was, but it was doubly so with her. First, it was only prostitutes or women that were outcasts who went to the well at that time of the day. Secondly, they would never speak to a man. So then they had a marvellous, religious theological discussion.

"Our father says you should worship in this mountain here." (They were right next to it, it is Mount Gerizim.) "You say they should worship at Jerusalem." Our Lord Jesus listened to it all and then just said to her, "Fetch your husband." She sort of flummoxed and flustered a bit, then she said, "I do not have a husband." "Yes," said the Lord Jesus, "you have said true. You had five and the one you now have is not your husband."

In a single moment the whole façade fell down like a pack of cards. It was not done in the religious way, the Pharisaical way, hauling some woman into the presence of the Lord to be dealt with, taken in the very act. "What should we do, stone her? That is what the law of Moses said." It all began with a request on His part. You see the testimony of Jesus? Out of this extraordinary meeting came one of the most wonderful things in the Gospel according to John—what true worship is. It is neither here nor there but in the Spirit.

Raising Lazarus

We will jump over chapters and chapters until we come to John 11. Here is one of the greatest mysteries of all, the mystery of the death of Lazarus. They besought the Lord Jesus to come, but He deliberately stayed away. He did not come at first. He knew exactly what He was going to do; He was going to raise Lazarus from the dead. He deliberately stayed away until it was absolutely certain. His death was certified and clear to everyone; it was not just a fainting fit. He was in the tomb, the stone was rolled over it, and it was sealed. The whole thing was certain.

Then the Lord came, and you know how Mary and Martha broke their hearts at His feet, and how the Lord Jesus said, "I am the resurrection and the life." Then the most extraordinary thing of all happened, and now this is the testimony of Jesus. Suddenly the Lord Jesus began to cry. It is, of course, the shortest verse in the Bible: John 11:35, "Jesus wept." It is the shortest verse in the Bible and it is the most profound mystery in the whole Bible because the Lord Jesus knew that He was going to raise Lazarus. Why then did He weep? The Lord Jesus, with His heart so sensitive, so compassionate, so sympathetic, knew what He was going to do with Lazarus. It was the whole thing of what had happened to man that broke upon the Lord Jesus. Man was never made for death. He was never made for all this corruption, and death and misery and emptiness. Suddenly it just overwhelmed the Lord Jesus, the misery of it all, the unhappiness of it all.

God never intended death in His scheme of things as we know it. Jesus wept and then He raised Lazarus. In that incident you have been introduced into the holiest place of all, and I defy anyone to understand it. There you are face-to-face with the kind of Person God is.

I will put it in another word from another Gospel. Perhaps it sounds sentimental, but if the Lord Jesus had not said it perhaps it would be. "Not even a sparrow falls to the ground without your Father." Think about that. It does not mean that God is sentimental, but it means that everything that happens in this groaning, misery-struck creation touches God—every aeroplane crash, every train crash, every bereavement, every sickness, every cruelty to children, every kind of cruel act to animals, whatever it is, animal to animal, human being to human being. In this sin-struck world, God is sensitive to the whole thing. You have it in these two words: "Jesus wept." This was not what God intended. This is not what God purposed. This was not that for which mankind or this creation was made. It was something altogether different to this.

The Impact of the Presence of Jesus

I have only taken a few examples from the Gospel of John to show you a little of what I believe the testimony of Jesus means. It was not just something to do with what He proclaimed. It was not only the truth He proclaimed and not only the action that He performed; it was His very presence that made the powerful and incisive impact upon this world. Sometimes the Lord Jesus did not have to say a single word. In John 8:3–9, a great mob, all very respectable religious leaders, came to the Lord Jesus hauling some miserable woman, flinging her at His feet. "Now," they said, "we have caught her in the very act. The law of Moses says, 'She should be stoned; what do You say?'"

He never answered a word—no sermon on the mount, no great platitudes about turning the other cheek, not a word. He just bent down and started to write on the ground, and we do not know what He wrote; He just doodled in the sand. One by one they went out from the eldest to the youngest. It was Dr. Campbell Morgan who said, "They went out from the eldest to the youngest because the eldest had the most sin and had lived the longest." Out they went, one by one. That is what I mean when I said it is not just the truth He proclaimed nor the action that He performed; it was His very presence.

When He stood before Pilate, He answered not a word and out of the heart of that hardened Gentile governor came the words, almost wistful: "What is truth?" "What is reality?" It was torn out of Him. Some people think it was sarcasm. I do not. It was the presence of Jesus; it was the testimony of Jesus. He was there.

Have you ever found that? Surely every one of us who has known the Lord in some little measure, whenever we have really touched Him, things have just been different when He has come near to us. When He has spoken with us, when some new light has come to us from the Word of God, the truth has set us free. "You shall know the truth and the truth shall set you free." Isn't that so? It is the testimony of Jesus. It was what He was in the final analysis. He not only bore testimony to the life of God which God was giving to man, He was that life, and it was that life which was the light. The light that the Lord Jesus gave is an altogether different kind of light. It is not the tree of the knowledge of good and evil; it is the tree of life. It was not just something in the mind that says this is wrong and that is right, but it was a kind of life that became light. You have it in John 1:4: "In him was life and the life was the light of men."

The Light of the World

Again, John 8:12 says: "I am the light of the world: he that followeth me shall not walk in the darkness, but shall have the light of life." Think of that. It is the most extraordinary phrase: "the light of life." It is not the light of intelligence but the light of life. It is just this that the Lord Jesus had. If you and I had wanted to sum it all up, I think I would sum it up in the words of the apostle John in the first letter of John 5:11a: "For this is the testimony." We read it normally, "This is the witness that God has given to us." I will put it in the older way: "And this is the testimony that God hath given unto us. He hath given unto us eternal life and this life is in His Son. He that hath the Son hath the life; he that hath not the Son of God hath not the life" (v. 12).

In verses 19–20 it says: "And we know that we are of God and the whole world lieth in the evil one. And we know that the Son of God is come, and hath given us an understanding, that we know him that is true, [real] and we are in him that is true, even in his Son Jesus Christ. This is the true God, and eternal life."

The testimony of Jesus in the ultimate analysis, in the final analysis is that the life of God, eternal life, the very life of God Himself was in Him. When you and I receive Him, when we are born of God, that life comes into us, and a union takes place. Later, we will take this further because it is bound up with the lampstand and the lampstand is bound up with the church. But it all comes back to this in its beginnings that first of all life was in Him and then through His death and resurrection it came to us. Then we have been joined to Him and He to us. Therefore, if I am joined to Him and He to me and if you are joined to Him and He to you, then something has happened between us. We are all in the same Christ and the same Christ is in all of us. We all have got the same life and the same life is in all of us. We are born of God into a new family. We have become members of Christ and one of another.

The Cherubim

Again, it was that life which was withheld from man when he fell. You have it in the very simple words of Genesis 3:22:

> And the Lord God said, Behold, the man is become as one
> of us, to know good and evil; and now, lest he put forth his
> hand, and take also of the tree of life, and eat, and live for
> ever—therefore the Lord God sent him forth from the garden
> of Eden, to till the ground from whence he was taken. So he
> drove out the man; and he placed at the east of the garden
> of Eden the Cherubim, and the flame of a sword which
> turned every way, to keep the way of the tree of life.

From that time when man fell and life was withheld from him, the Cherubim became the symbol of the divine veto. Whether you know this or you do not, it is a fact that in every great civilisation in the world some form of the Cherubim has existed—from the great Chinese winged dogs, to the winged lions of Assyria, to those of the great Incas, to the sphinx of Egypt. This idea has spread throughout the whole world and permeated the whole of civilisation. These fierce creatures are the ones that guard the way to the gods in mythology. But we know that the Cherubim are a symbol of divine veto. Eternal life is withheld by God from the likes of you and me.

The Veil of the Tabernacle

Later on came another symbol which was even more dramatic in its content—the veil of the tabernacle. It was a great heavy veil that divided the Holy of holies from the holy place, and on that veil were woven in embroidered work Cherubim. It was the divine veto. None of us can obtain the life of God. That veil was only removed when the Lord Jesus Christ sacrificed Himself. He sacrificed His own sinless and incorruptible life on the cross for our sin and then in His resurrection by the Holy Spirit He offered Himself to us as the very life of God, as life eternal. That moment the Lord Jesus offered Himself, His perfect life, as a sacrifice to God for our sins the veil in the temple with those embroidered Cherubim was torn in two from top to bottom by the hand of God. The way was opened. God was offering this life again to men and women by His Son. The divine veto has been lifted. I say that is wonderful! Listen to the simplicity of the words, but oh, the experience and agony behind them, the years of preparation from eternity—He that believeth on the Son of God hath eternal life.

Or again, listen to the words of the Lord Jesus: "He that eateth My flesh and drinketh My blood hath life in himself" (see John 6:53).

When we next see a picture of heaven in Revelation, chapters 4 and 5, which for some is a very involved passage but when understood is one of the most glorious passages in the whole Bible, a glorious and dramatic change has taken place. Now instead of the Cherubim acting as guards to the way of life, withholding it from man and barring the way to man, suddenly they become worshipping ushers to redeemed men and women, a whole innumerable multitude of the redeemed, ten thousand times ten thousand and thousands upon thousands pouring in, and the Cherubim no longer barring the way but ushering them in. First, they begin with the elders the song, and finally they say, "Amen." That is the testimony of Jesus. That is it; that God in Christ has finally and forever triumphed.

Here we are. We are in the history of it, but think of it. If you had lived in Abraham's time you would have been much farther back, but there was no difference. He saw Christ's day and rejoiced. We are toward the end of this age, this glorious age, this age of the grace of God. Now then, we still know something of a world that is upside down. We still know something of inverted values. We still know something of a world that is founded on a lie. We still know something of a life-blood that is poisoned. We still know something of a meaningfulness that is lost. It is all around us; it is on every side. We are in the world but we are no longer part of it. We have been delivered from the power of darkness and translated into the kingdom of the Son of God's love. We are still here and in the wisdom of God, unless He comes, we must all die. We have all still got to experience something of that which was never intended to be part of this creation and which the sacrifice of our Lord Jesus Christ has abolished. But that is why the glorious promise is to us: changed in the twinkling of an eye, the dead in

Christ rising first and we who are alive and remain caught up to be with Him. It is all so wonderful! It is the testimony of Jesus.

The Bride Adorned for Her Husband

Sometimes it is very hard for us to believe that God has got the final word in this, that the ultimate triumph is Christ's, but it is, and that is why we have the book of Revelation. There are martyrs under the altar; think of it. Some sort of lid is lifted up and a cry comes out: "How long?" The voice comes back with absolute calmness from heaven: "Till the number of the martyrs is fulfilled" and the lid is put down. Now for us it seems, "Oh, dear, dear, dear." But it is comforting in a way; it is all wholly according to the sovereign plan of God. It is all in hand, the triumph is His, absolutely His. So you get this book with its great conflict, its satanic antagonism, its world system of evil, antichrist here, a worldwide counterfeit church there, everything seeming to go wrong. Finally, the last picture is of the city coming down out of heaven adorned as a bride for her Husband. The ultimate triumph is with God. This is the testimony of Jesus, and this is the testimony that you and I hold. We hold it—the testimony of Jesus. "They that hold the testimony of Jesus."

Thank God, the Lord Jesus, our glorified and triumphant Head has gone into the heavens and is seated at the right hand of God the Father beyond the reach of Satan, beyond the reach of all the powers of darkness and evil. He is there; He has triumphed and now it is our place to hold the testimony of Jesus without compromising, whatever the cost or whatever the price, until finally we see the day of God's ultimate triumph dawn—and we shall.

I do hope the Lord has helped you to understand a little that is involved in this difficult subject. I hope the Lord will help you understand a little of what this phrase, the testimony of Jesus means.

Shall we pray:

Beloved Lord, we do lift up our hearts to Thee, and we praise Thee for that testimony of Thine. Lord, there would be none of us here were it not for the way that Thou didst come into this world and the way that Thou didst give Thyself for us. Now Lord, we pray that we may be given divine illumination by Thy Spirit upon these things that as we search Thy Word and as we seek Thee, Lord, so it may dawn upon us something of the meaning of this phrase. Illuminate us, Lord, by Thy Spirit we pray, and we ask it in the name of our Lord Jesus Christ. Amen.

4.
The Testimony of Jesus and the Church

Revelation 1:2

John who bare witness of the word of God, and of the testimony of Jesus Christ, even of all things that he [John] saw.

Revelation 1:9

I John, your brother and partaker with you in the tribulation and kingdom and patience which are in Jesus, was in the isle that is called Patmos, for the word of God and the testimony of Jesus.

Revelation 12:17

And the dragon waxed wroth with the woman, and went away to make war with the rest of her seed, that keep the commandments of God, and hold the testimony of Jesus.

Revelation19:10

And I fell down before his feet to worship him. And he saith unto me, See thou do it not: I am a fellow-servant with thee and with thy brethren that hold the testimony of Jesus: worship God: for the testimony of Jesus is the spirit of prophecy.

I Corinthians 1:4–9

I thank my God always concerning you, for the grace of God which was given you in Christ Jesus; that in everything ye were enriched in him, in all utterance and all knowledge; even as the testimony of Christ was confirmed in you: so that ye come behind in no gift; waiting for the revelation of our Lord Jesus Christ; who shall also confirm you unto the end, that ye be unreprovable in the day of our Lord Jesus Christ. God is faithful, through whom ye were called into the fellowship of his Son Jesus Christ our Lord.

(These are all the references there are to this phrase the testimony of Jesus or the testimony of Christ. There are a number of others that we will compare with it. In the margin of some of your versions you will notice that it is translated mystery.)

I Corinthians 2:1

And I, brethren, when I came unto you, came not with excellency of speech or of wisdom, proclaiming to you the testimony of God.

II Timothy 1:8

Be not ashamed therefore of the testimony of our Lord, nor of me his prisoner: but suffer hardship with the gospel according to the power of God.

Revelation 1:5

And from Jesus Christ, who is the faithful witness, the firstborn of the dead, and the ruler of the kings of the earth.

(We do not have the word testimony, but we have the word that is so closely related to it, witness or testifier.)

Revelation 3:14

These things saith the Amen, the faithful and true witness, the beginning of the creation of God.

The seven points which we have considered are all bound up with this phrase *the testimony of Jesus*. Unfortunately, in some of the modern, colloquial versions the meaning of this little phrase is entirely obscured. It appears for the most part in the book of Revelation and elsewhere only a few times. It is not the testimony or witness that we bear *to* Jesus, but it is the testimony that the Lord Jesus Himself bore. It was not merely that the Lord Jesus defined for us God's true character; He Himself in Himself expressed that character. In other words, it is not just simply that He drew a picture for us in words of what God was like. We see God in flesh and blood in the Lord Jesus. *That* is the testimony of Jesus.

Or again, we can say that it is not just that He proclaimed God's eternal and original purpose for mankind. It is more than a proclamation. It is perfectly true that again and again the Lord Jesus by word explained something of what was in God's heart in the beginning, in the creation of this world and in the creation of man. However, He did far more than that. Even in the most practical circumstances, the most concrete situations of life down here on this earth, He revealed to us in Himself what God's eternal purpose is all about. He did more than that; He realised in Himself that purpose so that we can truly say the eternal purpose of God centres in and is summed up in our Lord Jesus Christ. That is what the testimony of Jesus means.

Again, we can say that He did not merely preach to us God's redeeming love and salvation. He is Himself the very embodiment of divine love, of Love incarnate. He is Himself the salvation of all God's people. It is not only that He *gives* something, but that He *is* something. It is not only that He *acted*, but that He *was*. That is the testimony of Jesus. He not only pointed us to the way back to God, but He was and is Himself the means and the way back to God. We could sum it all up very simply in this way. We can say that the Lord Jesus not only *gave* light; He *was* the light. He not only *gave* life; He *was* the life. He not only *loved*; He *was* love. That is the testimony of Jesus.

This world, in its darkness, its perversion, its corruption, its blindness, and its alienation from God, is founded on a lie that is woven into the very fabric of human society. The world is built basically on a lie, and it was into that world the Lord Jesus came, not only to proclaim truth, but to reveal truth, to be the truth. Thus, it was not only His words but His very presence.

We have looked at the Gospel of John and seen how John takes the eight great claims that the Lord Jesus makes, all the great I AMs, then the eight signs, and many other incidents, all of which He uses to set forth what we call the testimony of Jesus. Therefore, we see that the Lord Jesus is not just doing this and doing that, working miracles for the sake of miracles. But by His very presence He is dynamiting a whole kind of society, dynamiting a whole kind of world, a whole world order, a system that has come to be accepted, a philosophy that is in the very being of man. He, by Himself, by His very presence, dynamites the whole thing. That is the testimony of Jesus that we see supremely in the cross when He gave His life for us.

That is why you have that wonderful little word that perhaps few of us have really understood: "There is one God, one mediator also between God and men, himself man, Christ Jesus, who gave himself a ransom for all; the testimony to be borne in its own times" (1 Timothy 2:5–6). There you have it. It was the testimony which He bore in due time, supremely in the giving of Himself a ransom for us all, the Mediator, the middle Man between God and fallen humanity, fallen humanity and God. That is the testimony of Jesus.

The Testimony of Jesus Vested in the Church

When the Lord Jesus was exalted to the right hand of the Father, that testimony of His was committed to the church. In other words, the testimony of Jesus—it is not too strong a word to use— is vested in the church on earth, the church ourselves.

Acts 1:1—"The former treatise I made, O Theophilus, concerning all that Jesus began both to do and to teach." I want you to underline that little word <u>began</u>. The former treatise, the Gospel according to Luke, "I made O Theophilus, concerning all that Jesus began both to do and to teach." The book of Acts is the continuation of the doing and the teaching of our Lord Jesus

Christ. Of course, we have got it all in the epistles; it all came out of this. He continued to do and to teach but through what? How? Through His body. So we could say that the book of Acts is the continuation of the testimony of Jesus, the Head, through the body, His church. So you find in the book of Acts a glorious continuation of the testimony and it starts with these very words: "Ye shall receive power, when the Holy Ghost is come upon you: and ye shall be witnesses unto me both in Jerusalem, and in all Judea and in Samaria, and unto the uttermost part of the earth" (Acts 1:8 KJV).

Holding the Testimony of Jesus

Again, I think we ought to very carefully note this little phrase which is very easy to pass over—"holding the testimony of Jesus."

> ... and hold the testimony of Jesus;
> Revelation 12:17b

> ... thy brethren that hold the testimony of Jesus.
> Revelation 19:10b

This word hold is just a normal word, *have*, and I believe some of the versions put it that way: "have the testimony of Jesus." This means that the testimony of Jesus has been vested in these people; they hold it. They have it. It is not something, in one sense, which originated with them. It is not something that was initiated by them or in them; it was something they received. It is the testimony of the Lord Jesus which has been committed to their keeping. It has been vested in them; they hold the testimony of Jesus. That is why I am sad that in the modern, colloquial versions the meaning has been so completely obscured. It is very sad.

The Golden Lampstand

You have the same idea in the golden lampstand in Revelation 1:12. (This whole book is about the testimony of Jesus.) "And I turned to see the voice that spake with me. And having turned I saw seven golden candlesticks." The Authorised Version, the Revised Version and the American Standard Version say, "candlestick." But you will see in your margin that it is more correctly "lampstand."

In the very ancient world they did not have candles; they had little oil lamps. The golden lampstand in the tabernacle was a seven-branched stand into which fitted seven lamps; therefore, the correct term is lampstand. In the old world they would sometimes have a single stand with a lamp on top or maybe two lamps. (Some of you who have been to the British museum have seen them.) The one that was in the tabernacle, which has become for us so important in Scripture, had seven lamps. It was a lampstand. The stand holds the lamps, and the lamp contained the light. That throws a little bit of light upon why certain brothers known unto us in the past always used to insist on lampstand. That mystified some of us because we thought the whole thing about the lampstand was just simply that it had a candle and it gave light. However, the idea is something to do with holding the testimony of Jesus, and the perfect picture of it is the golden lampstand, which holds the lamps which give the light.

The Function of the Church in This World

The church's function in this world is testimony, and I do not think any Bible scholar would contradict this. She is not merely to proclaim the truth, but she is to express the truth in her own being. She is not just simply to shout the Word of God from the rooftops, but by her very existence, by her very way of life, by her very being, she is to reveal and to express the truth of God. The truth is in her. That is why the Spirit of God says in one of the epistles, "Ye are all light in the Lord" (Ephesians 5:8b). It is in you. You are not just giving it; it is in you. Jesus said, "Ye are the light of the world" (Matthew 5:14a). He said of Himself, "I am the light of the world" (John 8:12b). It has to be in us.

We can take it further than that. We are not only to preach Christ, to bear testimony to Him, testifying of Him, witnessing of Him in offices, schools, colleges, home, wherever we are amongst friends, out on the street, but we are to reveal Him in our being. That is the thing that counts. More damage has been done, has it not, by people who open their mouths unadvisedly about the Lord when their lives do not tally. In that office, in that home, wherever it is, the Lord's name is held in disrepute. This is what we mean by holding the testimony of Jesus—something of His authority and power, something of His risen life and fullness, something of His sensitive, tender compassion and love, something of His destiny and His glory to be expressed in and through us. That is what we mean by the church holding the testimony of Jesus. It is not just that we are a collection of religious people. No. Nor is it more than that—that we are a collection of people who are born again. Thank God we are born again believers, but that is not merely what God wants. It isn't so hard for the Lord to collect a group of people who are born again, but that is not the candlestick, that is not the lampstand. It is more than that. It is that people, united with Himself, disciplined by Himself, something of Himself inwrought into the very fibre of their being, express the authority and power of the name of Jesus. They become evidence of the risen life and fullness of the Lord Jesus Christ. They become, as it were, a vehicle, a vessel through which the compassion and love of God can be expressed not only to each other but to the world outside. There is a tremendous amount in Scripture about this once you see it. When you do not see it, it all seems a bit up in the air; but once you have seen it, the whole of the New Testament begins to live with a new meaning.

The Church in Corinth

For instance, take that little reference we read in 1 Corinthians 1:6: "Even as the testimony of Christ was confirmed in you." Why did Paul say this to that poor, pathetic church at Corinth with so much trouble, so much division, so much carnality amongst them? He starts off by refusing to accept things as they are. There are people who believe in a kind of realism: "Of course, you must accept things as they are." That is where they begin and they are always in a mess, and they leave the rest of us in a mess too. The apostle Paul is a realist of God's kind. He starts with the real position, which is in Christ and says the testimony of Christ has been confirmed in you. That is why you have got these gifts. That is why you are saved. That is why you are named with the name of Christ. The testimony of Christ has been confirmed in you. Then he goes on and says He will confirm it to the end too (v. 8). God is faithful, through whom you were called into the fellowship of his Son Jesus Christ our Lord (v. 9). He did not say fellowship *with* His Son but the fellowship *of* His Son.

What is this company of called-out people in Corinth? Are they to be just a collection of dear little believers, to be a collection of people proclaiming the gospel in a very simple way to the unsaved, to be a gathering of people who are concerned about their own transformation and sanctification? No, they are to be a lighted lampstand in that darkened and wicked and perverse city. There, they are to show, to give evidence of what God is like. There, they are to reveal something of the true character of God. They are to express in themselves something of God's eternal purpose. They are to show the love of God; that is where we get 1 Corinthians 13. They are to be the very embodiment of it, not, as I have often said, in a sentimental way with lovely rosy skies and twittering birds and all that kind of thing, but in the dark, seamy, vice-ridden city of Corinth. No doubt there were rosy skies and twittering birds if you looked for them, but there was also the dark and evil side of Corinth. However, the testimony of Christ is there.

The Angelic Hosts

In Ephesians 3:9–11 we see it again in another way: "And to make all men see what is the dispensation of the mystery which for ages hath been hid in God who created all things; to the intent that now unto the principalities and the powers in the heavenly places might be made known through the church the manifold wisdom of God, according to the eternal purpose which he purposed in Christ Jesus our Lord."

Here is a mystery, is it not? In other words, what the apostle Paul is saying is this: "Look here, you gathered-out saints, you sinners saved by grace in Ephesus, do you know what God is doing with you? He is actually educating the invisible angelic hosts through you. Do you know those dark experiences you sometimes go through, those inexplicable pressures that come to bear upon you? There is a whole host invisible to you that are all around you watching." In other words, the far greater company is not the seen company but the unseen company in every true church gathering. They are all there in their ranks watching. They are being instructed both by our falling and by our rising. God is teaching them.

Now, some of you may say, "Oh dear, this is just going a little too far." Well, I will give you two headaches. The first is 1 Peter 1:12: "To whom it was revealed, that not unto themselves, but unto you, did they minister these things [e.g. the prophets], which now have been announced unto you through them that preached the gospel unto you by the Holy Spirit sent forth from heaven; which things angels desire to look into."

There they all are—thousands of them here this evening. They are absolutely desiring to look into these things; God bless them. They have not been permitted as we have. This is our privilege, sinners saved by grace. Now we are becoming the flesh and blood vehicle through which God is allowing them to see.

I will give you another little phrase, which might make you think. And it is a rather inexplicable phrase in 1 Corinthians 11:10: "For this cause ought the woman to have a sign of authority on her head, because of the angels." Think that one out. People say there is no need for it; well, there is something to do with the angels. They are looking. They are watching. We do not understand what it is, what is happening or why, but there is some reason. In other words, this testimony of Jesus is not just to do with the flesh and blood things we can see all around us. Of course, it is a lot to do with Richmond, but it is not just to do with Richmond. It is to do with the unseen, both the fallen angelic hosts and those that are still servants of the Most High.

Once you begin to see this, the whole of your New Testament takes on a new complexion. 1 Thessalonians 1:7-8: "So that ye became an ensample to all that believe in Macedonia and in Achaia. (They did not just talk; they were ensamples to all who believe in Macedonia and in Achaia.) For from you hath sounded forth the word of the Lord, not only in Macedonia and Achaia, but in every place your faith to God-ward is gone forth."

That is the testimony. Something has happened. It is the faith and love which is in Jesus. These dear folk in Thessalonica had found it. They had become, not just by word something—thank God they had something to proclaim—but it was inside them corporately.

Then again, in the church in Rome, Romans 16:19-20

For your obedience is come abroad unto all men. I rejoice therefore over you: but I would have you wise unto that which is good, and simple unto that that which is evil. And the God of peace shall bruise Satan under your feet shortly.

That is what the Lord does. He takes fallen, sinful human beings that have been saved by His grace, joined to His own risen, triumphant Son, and through their very frail experience, their circumstances, the situations into which corporately He allows them to come, He bruises Satan under their feet. Thus, again and again all things work together for good to those who love God and walk according to His purpose.

We mentioned Acts 1:8: "Ye shall receive power, when the Holy Spirit is come upon you: and ye shall be My witnesses both in Jerusalem, and in all Judea and Samaria, and unto the uttermost part of the earth."

Bearing the Testimony of Jesus

It is not just a question of running around giving a little word of testimony on a platform here or a pulpit there. It is more than that. We are *bearing* the testimony. It is in us. It is perfectly right and true to say that we witness to Him, we speak of Him. But what good is that if the testimony is not in us? It is to be something much more than just a few personal words given concerning the Lord Jesus and His saving grace. That is the value and power of the church.

All authority hath been given unto me in heaven and on earth. Go ye therefore, and make disciples of all the nations, baptizing them into the name of the Father and of the Son and of the Holy Spirit: teaching them to observe all things

whatsoever I commanded you: and lo, I am with you always,
even unto the end of the world.
Matthew 28:19–20

There you have the whole thing. That is the testimony of Jesus. He has Himself borne it, and He has ascended to the right hand of God the Father. Now He tells us to go and says He is with us. The testimony of Jesus is committed to us.

Go ye into all the world, and preach the gospel.
Mark 16:15

When you look at it like that, I say there is something very wonderful about this whole matter of testimony. It is much more comprehensive than just preaching the truth, just defining the truth, either personally or corporately. It is something far more than that.

And they overcame him because of the blood of the Lamb, and
because of the word of their testimony.
Revelation 12:11

What was their testimony? Their testimony was that although they may have felt quite different, the facts concerning the Lord Jesus Christ were absolutely true and eternally so. That is how they overcame. That is why martyrs could die at the stake or die in the lion's arena. They overcame by the word of their testimony. In death they knew they were one with the Lord Jesus Christ. They proclaimed it. That is their testimony.

Union with Christ

The Lord Jesus said, "I and my Father are one." So we can say, "He and we are one," whatever we feel, whatever the circumstances, whatever the situation. Do not forget that the Lord Jesus said that before Gethsemane, before He went to the cross. "I and My Father are one." It was tested in Gethsemane to the nth degree, in a way that you and I will never be tested when the Lord Jesus said, "If this cup can pass from Me, nevertheless ..." That is the word of the testimony. "Nevertheless, not as I will, but as Thou wilt." There is union. So do not ever think that union means that the devil never comes to you and you never have doubts. The very presence of doubts can be just a glorious arena for the setting forth of the triumph of the Lord Jesus. It is the "nevertheless, not as I will, but as Thou wilt" that proclaims the victory.

The Prophetic Content of the Testimony of Jesus

> *I John, your brother and partaker with you in the tribulation and kingdom and patience which are in Jesus, was in the isle that is called Patmos, for the word of God and the testimony of Jesus.*
> *Revelation 1:9*

We have come a wide circle and here we are right back to it. What really then is the testimony of Jesus? Revelation 19:10 says: "The testimony of Jesus is the spirit of prophecy." For many years I have been mystified by this little phrase. I have always felt that somehow this was the most comprehensive thing said about the testimony of Jesus in the Bible. It is the last thing that is said about the testimony of Jesus, and as we would expect it gathers everything together. It is, as it were, the last word in the Bible about the testimony of Jesus. "The testimony of Jesus is the spirit of prophecy." I often wondered just what it meant. I read the context again and again and thought, what does that mean? Does it mean something to do with the prophets in the Old Testament? Or the prophets in the New Testament? Or is it something to do with John himself? Now if you look through your different versions, you will find that although basically they say the same thing, there is a wide variety of translations. "The testimony of Jesus is the breath of all prophecy," says Moffat. Someone else says, "Witness borne to Christ is the inspiration of the prophets." So it goes on and on.

This is how it has come to me only today, and, I believe if we look at it like this we will get nearer to the heart of the whole thing. The testimony of Jesus is prophetic in its content. You understand, of course, that the spirit of prophecy is not the Holy Spirit; it is the human spirit, the spirit in the sense of the influence, the import. The testimony of Jesus is prophetic in its content.

Think what we have said. That is comprehensive. In other words, what we are saying is this: the Lord Jesus is the divine prophet and in Him the Word of God is proclaimed and expressed. What we mean is this: the mind of God, the heart of God is expressed in the Lord Jesus Christ. It is prophetic. I think all of you know that prophecy is not predicting the future in its biblical sense. One aspect of prophecy is predicting and foretelling, but the main idea behind prophecy in the Bible is the revelation of the mind of God concerning His people or His ways. It can be the interpretation of history, it can be the explanation of the present, it can be the predicting of the future.

The Lord Jesus Interprets History

If you want to bear out what I have said go to the Old Testament and you will find some of the prophets talk about the past. They say to the people this and this and this is going to happen to you because of that and that and that. In other words, they are interpreting history. They are prophets.

The Lord Jesus is the supreme Prophet—King, Priest and Prophet. He is the One who interprets history. He is the One who explains the present. He is the One who predicts the future. Isn't that so? It is the testimony of Jesus.

When the Lord Jesus came into this world, suddenly the whole of history was interpreted. Suddenly the whole history of God's chosen people under the old covenant was explained. Why did God choose Abraham? Why did He yank him out of Ur of the Chaldees? Why did He, as it were, take him into a howling wilderness? Why did He bring him into a land which he never really gave him though He promised it? Why did He covenant with his son Isaac who was born in the most extraordinary circumstances? Why was Jacob chosen, not Esau? Why did God, the angel of His presence, wrestle with Jacob and change him into Israel? Why did Joseph go down into Egypt? Why was Moses hidden in the bulrushes? Why did God bring ten plagues upon the Egyptian people, the greatest civilisation of the ancient world? Why did He deliver that poor tribe of slaves out of Egypt? Why did He open the Red Sea? Why did He go before them in a pillar of cloud by day and a pillar of fire by night? Why did Sinai smoke with fire? Why did the voice of God sound like a trumpet? Why were the Ten Commandments given to this strange people? How odd of God to choose the Jews! Why did God do all this? Why is the whole of the Old Testament history and revelation summed up in a few words in the last book of the Old Testament—"Jacob I have loved"? (Malachi 1:2). God sent these gainsaying, contradicting, rebellious people into captivity twice and brought them back twice. Why did God do it all?

I say, there is really no explanation until Jesus came. When Jesus was born of the royal line of David, suddenly the whole of history was explained. He explained what the Quakers used to call the bad seed and the good seed, why Cain was a murderer and why Abel was accepted. It was the Lord Jesus that was the explanation of it all by His very presence.

The Lord Jesus Explains the Present

Oh, but it is much more than that. Why did the Lord Jesus face the whole system of the temple with its priesthood, its sacrifices, its many orders and ranks, Levites, priests, its magnificent temple, its services, its holy days, its fast days and everything else? That whole system came into collision with Him. That whole system shut out a blind man who had been given his sight, and excommunicated him. What does the Lord Jesus do? He goes and finds the man and says to him, "I am the door; by Me if any man enter in, he shall be saved." It was the explanation of the present.

"You have made My Father's house a den of thieves," when He called it "a house of prayer for all nations." It is the explanation of the present.

When you see that wicked evil man, Caiaphas, outwardly so pious, so good, so respectful, so religious, and his aged and more vile father-in-law, Annas, representing the whole of the religious world of its day—and then you see Jesus. It is an explanation of the present—religion and life.

The Lord Jesus Predicts the Future

The Lord Jesus is the explanation of, the prediction or foretelling of, the significance of the future. He explains the future. Death? Death has lost its sting. One day the dead in Christ are going to rise and we which are alive and remain are going to be caught up together with Him. These poor old bodies that we have are going are going to have redemption bodies one day. It is all foretold. It is the Lord Jesus that has given the significance. If Jesus had not been raised from the dead, our faith is vain. He is the significance of it all. He is coming back and with Him is coming the kingdom.

That is the testimony of Jesus; it is prophetic in its content. You and I hold this testimony. It has been entrusted to us. It is prophetic in its content. What I am trying to say is simply this: God is not just interested in getting people together to come to Bible studies and prayer meetings and to go out on the street evangelising. That is not merely what God is interested in. He wants that, but there is something of far, far greater significance than that. He wants that to be just, as it were, the overflow of something else much deeper and fuller. That deeper and fuller thing is this: the testimony of Jesus. In other words, what God wants to do is to be able to interpret history through His church, explain the present through His church, and give significance to the future through His church, if necessary sometimes predict it. That is what I say the churches ought to be.

What a tragedy when we look around at the Christian world and see what has happened! It is cluttered up with all kinds of little things—petty and narrow. The testimony of Jesus is the explanation of why the Lord would plunge a company of believers into all kinds of inexplicable things and experiences. That is why He will take this one and that one within a company and do it with them personally that He might show forth something. Then history has meaning.

It is exactly so in church history, no matter where you turn. The Waldensians, when it was a real movement of the Spirit of God, explained what God was doing. It is the same with the Reformation. When you think of the way the Lord engineered all kinds of things so that politically, economically, everything was right for the Reformation. Wycliffe was the forerunner and John Huss was another before that man we call Martin Luther appeared on the scene and burst the thing wide open. The interpretation of history is prophetic in its content. It is the testimony of Jesus.

I hope this gives you some little inkling of what the testimony of Jesus is. It is prophetic in its nature. That does not mean that we all just become prophets. Would to God we all were! It would be a wonderful thing. It does not only mean that. It means that our life together is prophetic. It is the revelation of the mind of God. Everything is according to His mind, everything is the expression of His will; it is prophetic. So it is not just what we say but what we are.

The Testimony in the Old Testament

In the Old Testament we see something of this typified in the tabernacle. Let us go back to it for a moment. First of all, I think you all must have read again and again the phrase *the testimony* in the Old Testament. Here are two examples of it:

> And thou shalt put into the ark the testimony which I shall give thee.
> Exodus 25:16

> And he gave unto Moses, when he had made an end of communing with him upon mount Sinai, the two tables of the testimony, tables of stone written with the finger of God.
> Exodus 31:18

In the Old Testament, the two tables of stone written with the finger of God were *the* testimony.

Then in the New Testament: John 1:1: "In the beginning was the Word." There you have it—the testimony of Jesus. "And the Word was with God, and the Word was God."

Those two tables of stone, those Ten Commandments, are the moral law of God. In other words, although to us they seem so negative, they are the expression of the kind of life which is in God. Of course, it is all summed up in this word from Deuteronomy and spoken again in the New Testament by the Lord Jesus: "Thou shall love the Lord Thy God with all thy soul, with all thy strength and with all thy might and thou shall love thy neighbour as thyself." The Ten are summed up like that, and that is the testimony.

Think of the Lord Jesus. He is God's moral law. Negatively— "Thou shalt not." Did He sin in one single way? Did He fall short in one single way? Positively—"Thou shall love the Lord thy God with all thy soul, with all thy strength and with all thy might and love thy neighbour as thyself." Did He do both? Absolutely! However, the testimony of Jesus is much more than the Ten Commandments. Can I put it reverently? It is the Word of God written with the finger of God. That is the Lord Jesus.

The Ark of the Testimony

The next phrase you will find is the ark of the testimony. One reference is in Exodus 26:33: "And thou shalt hang up the veil under the clasps, and shalt bring in thither within the veil the ark of the testimony."

This ark of the testimony was a box made of acacia wood which is like cedar wood. It never corrupts; it never rots. It was overlaid with pure gold so that you could not see the wood. All you could see was the gold. What scripture do you think we can get from that? Who is the ark of the testimony within which the Word of God resides?

And the Word became flesh, and dwelt among us (and we
beheld his glory, glory as of the only begotten from the Father),
full of grace and truth.
John 1:14

No man hath seen God at any time; the only begotten Son,
who is in the bosom of the Father, he hath declared him."
The perfect humanity of the Lord Jesus, the perfect deity of the
Lord Jesus—that is the ark of the testimony.
John 1:18

Veil of Testimony

We find a reference to the veil of the testimony in Leviticus 24:3:
"Without the veil of the testimony."

This is the veil that parted man from God and God from man.
It was the veil that separated the holy of holies from the holy place.
It divided the tent of meeting.

Can you think of any scripture relating to this? Most of you
ought to have thought of Hebrews 10:19–20. Here is the ark of
the covenant, the ark of the testimony in another way: "Having
therefore, brethren, boldness to enter into the holy place by the
blood of Jesus, by the way which he dedicated for us, a new and
living way, through the veil, that is to say, his flesh."

In other words, the ark speaks of the perfect being of the Lord
Jesus, but the veil speaks of His sacrifice. He was wounded for us,
opened, torn so that we can go through—the veil of the testimony.

The Tabernacle of Testimony

Finally, in this Old Testament picture we find it all summed up in the tabernacle of the testimony. Numbers 9:15 says: "And on the day that the tabernacle was reared up the cloud covered the tabernacle, even the tent of the testimony: and at even it was upon the tabernacle as it were the appearance of fire, until morning"— the tabernacle of the testimony.

In other words, the first thing you and I would have seen if we had been living under the old covenant was the tabernacle. As soon as we had gone into the outer court we would have looked beyond the altar, beyond the laver, and we would have seen the tabernacle. That was the tabernacle of the testimony. Then, beyond that was the veil of the testimony, beyond that the ark of the testimony, and within that was the testimony.

What scripture could we give for the tabernacle of the testimony? The one I thought of amongst many is in Ephesians 1:22: "And he put all things in subjection under his feet, and gave him to be head over all things to the church, which is his body, the fullness of him that filleth all in all."

There you have the testimony of Jesus. We hold the testimony of Jesus, like the tabernacle; it is within us. You go through the tent of meeting, through the veil to the ark, and it is within the ark.

The Symbol of the Testimony of Jesus

In the Bible, what is the supreme symbol of the testimony of Jesus? Of all the furniture in the tabernacle or the temple the piece that was selected finally through the Word of God as the supreme picture or symbol of the testimony of Jesus was the golden lampstand. I think you all know that; it does not matter where you look in the Bible. This golden lampstand may not appear a lot of times, but when it does, it is always significant. You first find it in Exodus 25:31–40. It is of pure gold, a beaten work of one piece.

In chapter 27:20 we read about the oil and we are told it is to burn continually; it is never to go out day or night unto all generations. That lamp is never to be allowed to go out ever. Also, we are told about the oil, how it is to be crushed and how it is to be prepared. It was to be pure olive oil of the finest kind.

The Golden Lampstand in Zechariah

When we take a leap over the tabernacle and the temple and that whole period of history to Zechariah 4, we find the prophet talking about recovery, rebuilding. It is all to do with the rebuilding of Jerusalem, the rebuilding of the temple, the recovery of the house of God, the reinstitution of the services and everything else. The prophet is very burdened and bothered, and what does he see? In a vision he sees a golden lampstand. He does not see a house; he sees a golden lampstand and two olive trees on either side that feed it with gold, literally. You will notice that in the modern versions they added the word, golden oil, because it does not seem to make sense. The two olive trees empty gold out of themselves into the lampstand. Poor old Zechariah does not quite understand it. He knew a lot about the house of God, but he could not understand this and he asked the angel, "What does it mean?" The angel completely ignored his question about the two olive trees, which were the two things that so interested Zechariah. Instead, he said, "This is the word of the Lord to Zerubbabel, 'Not by might, nor by power, but by my Spirit, saith the Lord of Hosts. This great mountain shall become a plane and the top stone shall be brought forth with shouts of grace, grace unto it'" (see Zechariah 4:6–7). In other words, the whole thing is to do with building, with the recovery and the completion of this building.

Then he said, "They shall rejoice; the seven eyes of the Lord when they see the plummet line in the hands of Zerubbabel. The plummet line is all to do with building according to plan. You do not need a plummet line if you do not bother about plans, but if you are very bothered about plans you need a plummet line. Then it just says: "The hands of Zerubbabel have laid the foundation of this house; his hands shall also finish it."

Zechariah, not to be out done, says, "What about the olive trees?" "Oh," said the angel, "don't you know what those are? They are the two anointed ones who stand by the Lord of the whole earth." In other words, these are Zerubbabel and Joshua—king and priest, the two great ministries.

We are made kings and priests unto God. Isn't it interesting that the golden lampstand comes into view just at that point in the history of God's people, just before the coming of the Messiah, just when it was absolutely necessary for the house of God to be completed? It is the testimony of Jesus.

The Seven Golden Lampstands

The next time we find the golden lampstand we take another leap. In Revelation chapters 1, 2, 3 we see that a tremendous amount has happened. The whole point of history has been reached and fulfilled in the coming of the Lord Jesus Christ in His death and resurrection. Now, the risen, ascended, triumphant Lord is in the midst of seven golden lampstands, and He is talking to each one of them. He has a message for each one of His lampstands. Then we find they are seven churches. Don't you think all of that is of tremendous significance?

The Two Witnesses

Take another leap and where do you come down? Revelation 11, and that is a mysterious chapter. There are the two witnesses and the temple, and the angel says, "Rise, and measure the outer court." Then you see the temple, the two witnesses, and there we are told these are the two olive trees and the two golden lampstands. It is the testimony of Jesus. These two witnesses, whoever they are or whatever they represent, are slain at the end of the age and their bodies lie dead until God raises them up from the dead and they ascend into heaven. It is the testimony of Jesus again, the golden lampstand.

The New Jerusalem

Take another leap to see just where you get the golden lampstand. In Revelation 21 and 22 you have got the holy city of God, the New Jerusalem, the bride, the wife of the Lamb. If you look very carefully into those two chapters you find that the city is one great lampstand. It has many figures. We see it first as a wife, then as a city; we see pearls and precious stones, all kinds of things, but it is pure gold like unto pure glass, transparent as glass. We are told in verse 11 of chapter 21 that her light is like unto a precious stone, a jasper stone, and that word *light* is the word "light-giver, light-bearer." It is the word for sun or moon.

Then in verse 23 you will find this remarkable thing: "And the glory of God did lighten it;" so the flame of fire in the lamp is the glory of God. Then you read, "And the lamp thereof is the Lamb." So the glory of God is in the Lamb. Who is the Lamb? And where is the lamp? The Lamb is in the lampstand; the seven-fold lamp is Jesus, held by the stand. Verse 24 says, "The nations shall walk in the light thereof." There you have got it. It is the seven-branched golden lampstand, and that is the explanation of eternity to come. The nations shall walk in the light of it. It is the testimony of Jesus. It is not just something to do with time alone, but eternity.

I do not think it is hard for us to see that the lampstand is the symbol of the testimony of Jesus, the pure gold of His nature and character, the deep, inwrought travail and suffering out of which the lampstand is produced. It is a beaten work so that every branch is beaten out of it; not added, not soldered on or brazed on, but beaten out of one piece and then turned with deep, inwrought travail and sufferings to produce it. We can see it in the absolute unity of the whole thing, one piece. That is what it says, "It shall be of one piece." We can see it in the pure oil of the Spirit of life, and we can see it in the lighted oil, the light of His life. "In Him was life; and the life was the light of man" (John 1:4). I am the light of the world: he that followeth Me shall not walk in darkness, but shall have the light of life" (John 8:12). You have it all in the golden lampstand.

One of the Keys to the Whole Bible

If the Holy Spirit has been able to write anything into our hearts, the one thing we can be quite certain of is that though this phrase, the testimony of Jesus, does not occur a lot of times, it is one of the keys to the whole Bible. That is why this book of Revelation, the last book that sums up everything in the Bible, uses this term more than any other, *the testimony of Jesus*. Oh, if only God could do such a thing in us that we are consistent with holding the testimony of Jesus! All those works of darkness, all that belongs to the shadow, all that belongs to another system, to another world, oh, if we would only let the Holy Spirit deal with it. Of course, the church down here will always be a kind of melting pot, a place where the scum comes to the surface, the rubbish is cleared out, and all the rest of it. Of course, we do not expect a perfect church down here; we are not meant to. But oh that the testimony of Jesus could be held! That is what we shall be considering as we see the Lord in the midst of those seven golden lampstands speaking to each one and judging everything in relation to the holding of His testimony. Unto each one He says, "He that overcomes." It is all in relation to the testimony. May God give us all grace that by His life that is within us we might overcome and sit down with Him in His throne.

Shall we pray:

Lord, Thou hast spoken to us in the past year or two a number of times about this golden lampstand, and we have all been perplexed by it. Even when we understood quite a measure we have been concerned, Lord, as to whether we really understand it. We pray that by Thy Holy Spirit Thou would bring home to us the meaning of it, the testimony of Jesus. Burn it into our hearts, Lord. Light it with Thy finger upon the fleshy tables of our hearts. Let it get into us, Lord, and do its work individually and corporately.

Thou hast also spoken to us Lord, about those who can bear the ark of the testimony upon their shoulders. We remember that, Lord, and we pray that Thou wouldst help us to understand more of what it means to shoulder divine things, to hold the testimony of Jesus. Our beloved Lord, our greatest desire is that at the end we may be in the city and part of the bride; we may be in that lampstand in whose light the nations will walk. Oh God, give us grace we pray, every one of us, by Thy life within us, by Thy victory on Calvary, by Thy Holy Spirit to overcome and sit down finally with Thee. We ask it in the name of our Lord Jesus Christ. Amen.

5.
Holding the
Testimony of Jesus

Revelation 1:1–20

The Revelation of Jesus Christ, which God gave him to show unto his servants, even the things which must shortly come to pass: and he sent and signified it by his angel unto his servant John; who bare witness of the word of God, and of the testimony of Jesus Christ, even of all things that he saw. Blessed is he that readeth, and they that hear the words of the prophecy, and keep the things that are written therein: for the time is at hand.

John to the seven churches that are in Asia: Grace to you and peace, from him who is and who was and who is to come; and from the seven Spirits that are before his throne; and from Jesus Christ, who is the faithful witness, the firstborn of the dead, and the ruler of the kings of the earth. Unto him that loveth us, and loosed us from our sins by his blood; and he made us to be a kingdom, to be priests unto his God and Father; to him be the glory and the dominion for ever and ever. Amen. Behold he cometh with the clouds; and every eye shall see him, and they that pierced him; and all the tribes of the earth shall mourn over him. Even so, Amen.

I am the Alpha and Omega, saith the Lord God, who is and who was and who is to come, the Almighty.

I John, your brother and partaker with you in the tribulation and kingdom and patience which are in Jesus, was in the isle that is called Patmos, for the word of God and the testimony of Jesus. I was in the Spirit on the Lord's day, and I heard behind me a great voice, as of a trumpet saying, What thou seest, write in a book and send it to the seven churches: unto Ephesus, and unto Smyrna, and unto Pergamum, and unto Thyatira, and unto Sardis, and unto Philadelphia, and unto Laodicea. And I turned to see the voice that spake with me. And having turned I saw seven golden lampstands; and in the midst of the lampstands one like unto a son of man, clothed with a garment down to the foot, and girt about at the breasts with a golden girdle. And his head and his hair were white as white wool, white as snow; and his eyes were as a flame of fire; and his feet like unto burnished brass, as if it had been refined in a furnace; and his voice as the voice of many waters. And he had in his right hand seven stars: and out of his mouth proceeded a sharp two-edged sword; and his countenance was as the sun shineth in his strength. And when I saw him, I fell at his feet as one dead. And he laid his right hand upon me, saying, Fear not; I am the first and the last, and the Living one; and I was dead, and behold, I am alive for evermore, and I have the keys of death and of Hades. Write therefore the things which thou sawest, and the things which are, and the things which shall come to pass hereafter; the mystery of the seven

stars which thou sawest in my right hand, and the seven golden
lampstands. The seven stars are the angels of the seven churches:
and the seven lampstands are seven churches.

Revelation 21:9–18, 22–27

And there came one of the seven angels who had the seven bowls,
who were laden with the seven last plagues; and he spake with me,
saying, Come hither, I will show thee the bride, the wife of the Lamb.
And he carried me away in the Spirit to a mountain great and high,
and showed me the holy city Jerusalem, coming down out of heaven
from God, having the glory of God: her light was like unto a stone
most precious, as it were a jasper stone, clear as crystal: having a
wall great and high; having twelve gates, and at the gates twelve
angels; and names written thereon, which are the names of the twelve
tribes of the children of Israel: on the east were three gates; and on the
north three gates; and on the south three gates; and on the west three
gates. And the wall of the city had twelve foundations, and on them
twelve names of the twelve apostles of the Lamb. And he that spake
with me had for a measure a golden reed to measure the city, and the
gates thereof, and the wall there of. And the city lieth foursquare,
and the length thereof is as great as the breadth; and he measured
the city with the reed, twelve thousand furlongs: the length and
the breadth and the height thereof are equal. And he measured the
wall thereof, a hundred and forty and four cubits, according to the
measure of a man, that is, of an angel. And the building of the wall
thereof was jasper: and the city was pure gold, like unto pure glass …
And I saw no temple therein: for the Lord God the Almighty, and the

Lamb, are the temple thereof. And the city hath no need of the sun, neither of the moon, to shine upon it: for the glory of God did lighten it, and the lamp thereof is the Lamb. And the nations shall walk amidst the light thereof: and the kings of the earth bring their glory into it. And the gates thereof shall in no wise be shut by day (for there shall be no night there): and they shall bring the glory and the honor of the nations into it: and there shall in no wise enter into it anything unclean, or he that maketh an abomination and a lie: but only they that are written in the Lamb's book of life.

Revelation 22:3–5, 16–20

And there shall be no curse any more: and the throne of God and of the Lamb shall be therein: and his servants shall serve him; and they shall see his face; and his name shall be on their foreheads. And there shall be night no more; and they need no light of lamp, neither light of sun; for the Lord God shall give them light: and they shall reign for ever and ever … I Jesus have sent mine angel to testify unto you these things for [over] the churches. I am the root and the offspring of David, the bright, the morning star. And the Spirit and the bride say, Come. And he that heareth, let him say, Come. And he that is athirst, let him come: he that will, let him take the water of life freely. I testify unto every man that heareth the words of the prophecy of this book, If any man shall add unto them, God shall add unto him the plagues which are written in this book: and if any man shall take away from the words of the book of this prophecy, God shall take away his part from the tree of life, and out of the holy city, which are written in this book. *He who testifieth these things saith, Yea: I come quickly. Amen: come, Lord Jesus.*

We come now to the third and final study on the subject, "The Testimony of Jesus." I will take up one thing to refresh your memory from the last study we had, and that is the phrase in Revelation 19:10: "The testimony of Jesus is the spirit of prophecy." In that one sentence we have, as far as I can see, the most comprehensive statement in the whole Bible concerning this little phrase "the testimony of Jesus." It only occurs a few times, mostly in the book of Revelation, and a few times elsewhere. It has been obscured in some of our more modern, colloquial versions, but it is nevertheless a very, very important and significant phrase.

The Prophetic Nature of the Testimony of Jesus

What is the testimony of Jesus? It is not merely, or in a general way, our witnessing of Him. The testimony of Jesus is the testimony that He Himself bore, and it is not only a question of what He said or what He taught or the light He gave. It is much deeper than that. It is a question of what He was and is. That is the testimony of Jesus. He *is* the light of the world. It is not only that He gives light, but He is the light. In that lies, really, the testimony of Jesus.

The testimony of Jesus is the spirit of prophecy. That is, the testimony of Jesus is prophetic in its content, or in its import, or in its nature. What do we mean by that? Prophecy is not just predicting the future. It can be the interpretation of history, it can be the explanation of the present, it can be giving significance to the future, and it can be actually predicting or foretelling what the future holds. That is prophecy. It is the revelation of the mind of God in a given situation to given people.

The testimony of Jesus is prophetic in its content; He is the very revelation and expression of the mind of God. He is the interpretation of all history. He is the explanation of the present. He is the One who gives significance to the future whether future time or future eternity. He is the One through whom and by whom the future makes sense. That is the testimony of Jesus. That testimony which He bore, which He gave, has been vested and committed to us. That is why we get that little phrase in the book of Revelation: "holding the testimony of Jesus." We hold the testimony of Jesus; it is a very strange phrase. We hold it. We do not just give it; we hold it. It is something committed to us, something vested in us.

The Golden Lampstand

In our last study we ended on this matter of the golden lampstand. Of all the symbols used in the Old Testament, of all the furniture or vessels in the tabernacle or temple the one that supremely symbolised the testimony of Jesus was the lampstand all of gold. It is not candlestick as it says in the Authorised Version, but correctly, it is lampstand. In the ancient world it was a stand. Especially in the ancient Jewish world and Middle Eastern world, there was a stand and lamps were fitted into the stand. Sometimes there would be only one lamp. In Matthew 5:15 the Lord Jesus says, "Neither do men light a lamp, and put it under the bushel, but on the stand." In other words, it is a stand specially fitted with a moulded top fitting into which was a special little lamp, holding oil with a wick. Sometimes there were two, sometimes there were three, and sometimes there was one. The one in the tabernacle or temple had seven branches and held seven lamps that fitted into it. It is this golden lampstand that is taken as the supreme symbol of the testimony of Jesus in the Bible, and you find it all the way through.

The House of God

The first mention of lampstand is in Exodus 25 and Exodus 27. Then we take a great leap (apart from the fact that it was in the temple) to Zechariah 4. At this point of great crisis in the history of God's people, just at the point when the house of God had got to be rebuilt, just when the temple had got to be restored for the coming of the Messiah, a vision was given to a prophet called Zechariah. The vision is all to do with a golden lampstand and two olive trees on either side. Only then do we discover that this golden lampstand stands for the house of God and is actually a symbol of all this reconstruction and recovery and restoration and rebuilding.

The Spiritual House of God

When we take another great leap, we come to the New Testament. Now, a tremendous amount has happened. The Lord Jesus has come into the world; the Messiah has been born. He suddenly came to His temple, and the temple came into collision with the Messiah. They excommunicated a blind man so the Messiah excommunicated the temple and said, "I AM the door. By Me if any man enter in he shall be saved and shall go in and go out and shall find pasture." They crucified Him, the Lord of glory, and the Father raised Him on the third day. He ascended into heaven to the right hand of God the Father, and He obtained the promised Holy Spirit and poured Him forth. That brings us to the day of Pentecost when a spiritual house of God came into being, when living stones were produced by the action of the Holy Spirit. It was the golden lampstand, although it is not mentioned.

We jump over to Revelation chapters 1, 2 and 3 and we find that the Lord is in the midst of these golden lampstands. He is speaking to seven churches. These seven golden lampstands are seven churches.

We take another leap and we come to Revelation chapter 11, that mysterious chapter. First, we see the outer court of the temple, then we see the temple, then we see into the temple, then we read about two witnesses, and then we hear the strange words: "These are the two golden lampstands that stand before the Lord of the whole earth, and the two olive trees." Whether that signifies two prophets at the end of the dispensation, whether it is a company of the Lord's children who will be prophetic in their being, in their corporate existence—I do not mean a particular local company but worldwide—whatever it is, we do not know. What we do know is that this company or these two prophets draw out the antagonism of this world and the fury of Satan so that finally they are destroyed like their Master and raised up like their Master after three days, most remarkable, and ascended into heaven like their Master. I will leave that with you.

Then we take another leap to the end of the Bible to chapters 21 and 22. We find the golden lampstand there.

The Significance of the Lampstand

What is this golden lampstand? I think we all realise that it is filled with significance. The material out of which this golden lampstand was made was pure gold, the pure gold of the nature and character and life of Christ.

The second thing we notice is that it was beaten work. That is, the lampstand is produced out of inwrought travail and suffering. It is in the fellowship of His sufferings, in the filling up of the afflictions which have been left for us for His body's sake. It was beaten work, not each branch made separately and then brazed on or soldered on. Out of one piece of gold it is beaten and hammered and then turned and turned until seven branches appear out of one piece. That speaks of the travail of our Master, of our Lord, and of the inestimable privilege granted to us as children of God to enter into something of the fellowship of His sufferings. Paul said, "My little children, of whom I am again in travail." Again? He has been in it once before. "Of whom I am again in travail till Christ be fully formed in you all." Literally, it is "among you," not just one, but in you all—corporate (see Galatians 4:19).

It was of one piece, meaning it is absolute unity. The whole lampstand is of one piece. That speaks of the absolute unity of the Lord Jesus, the oneness of Christ into which we have been born by His Spirit.

Then, very careful instructions are given to us in Exodus 27:20 about the oil. The olives are to be the best olives, they are to be crushed, they are to be sieved, as it were, so that it is the finest of the oil for the lamp. We all know that the oil speaks of the Holy Spirit. It is the life, the pure oil of the Spirit of life, the Holy Spirit, the Spirit of Christ, the Spirit of God. So this lampstand is to contain the pure life of the Spirit of God, the risen life of Christ.

Then again, we are told in Exodus 27:20–21 that the lamp was to burn continually throughout all their generations; never was it allowed to go out. It was to be an everlasting light through day and through night. What does that speak of? That lighted oil speaks of the light of His life. "In Him was life, and the life was the light of men" (John 1:4). "He that followeth me shall not walk in the darkness but shall have the light of life" (see John 8:12). The Holy Spirit within us gives rise to light; His life gives rise to light. It is not the tree of the knowledge of good and evil which makes us independent of God, but the kind of knowledge that comes through the tree of life, which makes us dependent upon Him.

The Seven Golden Lampstands

Surely, therefore, it is of very great and real significance that the book of Revelation, which deals so much with the testimony of Jesus and the churches holding that testimony, should commence with the Lord in the midst of seven golden lampstands. It is an extraordinary vision, but we are all used to it unfortunately, so the impact of it does not come home to us. What an extraordinary vision for an apostle to have, to see His risen Lord glorified, triumphant, alive forevermore with the keys of death and hell in

His hands! What is He doing? He is standing in the midst of seven golden lampstands. They are in a perfect circle right around Him.

At first, the apostle does not realise that it is churches that are symbolized. He just sees the Lord in the midst of these seven golden lampstands; that is all. What is it really that we find represented here? It is this: the Lord is in the midst of those seven golden lampstands which represent seven local churches or the church in its practical expression on earth in time. He is judging everything in those churches in relation to their holding of this testimony. Everything in these seven churches is judged in the light of the testimony. You can see it quite clearly again and again as the Lord points to this that is wrong, to that which is wrong, and to the other that is wrong.

Then the word comes: "I will remove the lampstand out of its place." What does He mean? He is judging everything in relation to the testimony. In other words, these things amongst them— this Jezebel here, this problem here, this Nicolaitism here, this erroneous teaching there—all have bearing on the testimony of Jesus. "I will remove the golden lampstand out of its place." In other words, the church seemingly will continue. They will still have their prayer meetings, their Bible studies, and their evangelistic meetings. It will all seem to rumble on outwardly, but the testimony is gone; the testimony of Jesus has been removed. In God's sight it is no longer the church. Now, that is terrible, but that is precisely what we see in the first three chapters of Revelation.

Overcoming in Relation to His Testimony

What is the word that comes as the Lord puts His finger on this and that and the other? Again and again to every single church, whether commended or not, comes the word: "To him that overcometh." He is judging everything in relation to the holding of His testimony.

How many of you have been a little bewildered at what is promised to those that overcome? "He shall eat of the tree of life" (2:7). But surely if we are Christians we have eaten of the tree of life. "He shall not be hurt of the second death" (2:11). Well, we are not going to be hurt of the second death, are we? Just wait, you have overlooked something. It is the testimony of Jesus. The testimony of Jesus is the life of God given to us. He that overcometh is in it. To him that overcometh, he shall not be hurt of the second death. No death. Then it speaks about writing "My new name upon him" (2:17). "I will write upon him the name of the city of my God and the name of my God" (3:12). Finally, He says, "To him that overcometh shall I grant to sit down in My throne as I have sat down in My Father's throne" (3:21). It is the testimony. This means that this overcoming is all in relation to the testimony.

Chapter 2:5: "Remember therefore whence thou art fallen, and repent and do the first works; or else I come to thee, and will move thy lampstand out of its place, except thou repent."

I think that most of us have got the idea that if the lampstand were to be moved we should immediately feel it. I say that we must be very sensitive to the Spirit of God to know when the lampstand is gone. It is perfectly possible, and the whole of church history bears me out, for the lampstand to be withdrawn and the saints not even to realise it, so dull do we become, so insensitive do we become.

In chapter 2:16 we have the same thought. We are not told about the lampstand, but it is the same thing: "Repent therefore; or else I come to thee quickly, and I will make war against them with the sword of my mouth."

Chapter 3:3: "Remember therefore how thou hast received and didst hear; and keep it, and repent. If therefore thou shalt not watch, I will come as a thief, and thou shalt not know what hour I will come upon thee." Surely that is in connection with the removing of the lampstand.

Verse 16: "So because thou art lukewarm, and neither hot nor cold, I will spew thee out of my mouth." It is the same thought all the way through.

If you go back again to chapter 2:7 we read this: "To him that overcometh, to him will I give to eat of the tree of life, which is in the Paradise of God [garden of God]."

Verse 11: "He that overcometh shall not be hurt of the second death."

Verse 17: "To him that overcometh, to him will I give of the hidden manna, and I will give him a white stone, and upon the stone a new name written, which no one knoweth but he that receiveth it."

Verse 26–28: "And he that overcometh, and he that keepeth my works unto the end, to him will I give authority over the nations: and he shall rule them with a rod of iron, as the vessels of the potter are broken to shivers; as I also have received of my Father: and I will give him the morning star."

Chapter 3:5: "He that overcometh shall thus be arrayed in white garments: and I will in no wise blot his name out of the book of life, and I will confess his name before my Father, and before his angels."

Verse 12: "He that overcometh, I will make him a pillar in the temple of my God, and he shall go out thence no more: and I will write upon him the name of my God, and the name of the city of my God, the new Jerusalem, which cometh down out of heaven from my God, and mine own new name."

Verse 21: "He that overcometh, I will give to him to sit down with me in my throne, as I also overcame, and sat down with my Father in his throne."

We can see that this book of Revelation, which deals so much with the testimony of Jesus, begins with the Lord in the midst of seven golden lampstands that represent the church on earth and in time. He is judging everything in them in relation to their holding of His testimony. Even this word overcoming is all to do with the testimony of Jesus. The same book ends with the holy city of God, the New Jerusalem, the bride, the wife of the Lamb.

The City at the End of Revelation

When you read those last two chapters of the Bible, what does it signify? What do you understand? You have a most extraordinary picture of the most extraordinary things. One thing is that it is a city; but you have never heard of a city that is a woman. This city is a bride; this bride is the wife of the Lamb. Then, we find that this city is quite extraordinary because it is as high as it is broad as it is long. It is an absolute cube. Now, the holiest place of all was an absolute cube. In other words, the whole thought is this: there is no temple. It is the temple. In the Bible, in English there is just the word "temple," but in Greek and in Hebrew there is a different word, one word signifying the whole temple and the other signifying the sanctuary. That is the holiest place of all. That was the cube, foursquare. What does it mean? This bride, this wife of the Lamb, this city, this new Jerusalem is the sanctuary of God. It is the holiest place of all. It is the holy of holies.

However, there is something more extraordinary. You have never heard of a city which is hundreds and hundreds and hundreds of miles long and just the same many miles wide and just the same many miles high with only one street. It would be a most circuitous street; yet it says there is only one street in that whole city.

Then again, we are told that it is precious stone, yet we are told in the same breath that it is gold, transparent as glass. In other words, you can see through this enormous city from end to end; it is crystal clear. What does this all signify? I will tell you what it signifies. You will not find any church in it. You will not find any chapel in it. You will not find any synagogue in it. You will not find any temple in it. What is it? It signifies the final, absolute, gloriously eternal union between the Lord and His children. They have been fused together into an absolute unity never to be divorced. The bride and the Lamb are wed.

The city is like glass. God is in it and His light streams out through it. I have often said that when you take a clear, transparent electric light bulb, when the light is not on, you can see the bulb.

However, the moment you put the light on, the bulb is lost in a blaze of light. That is this city. As soon as the glory of God lights it, you do not see the city. All you can see is the glory of God; all you can see is the Lord Himself. It signifies this absolute union which God has longed for from the very beginning of time.

Of course, it is not our study here to speculate as to what is going to happen in the future. All we know is that the Bible begins with this great desire of God to be one with us and for us to be one with Himself. This great desire of God is to incorporate us into Himself—and that is the exact word—to make us a body, to incorporate us into Himself, and it ends with the accomplished fact. In other words, this city, this New Jerusalem, this bride, this wife of the Lamb signifies that the eternal purpose of God and the object of our redemption in time have both been fulfilled. Remember, God had a purpose before man fell. God's redeeming purpose was because man fell and therefore in this city we see both His purposes come together—His original purpose, His eternal purpose for us and the object of our redemption, His saving us together.

What is this city of God, this New Jerusalem, this bride, this wife of the Lamb, this sanctuary of God? It is one golden lampstand, that's all, and the lamp thereof is the Lamb and the light thereof is the glory of God. We find that in those two chapters, which I will point out to you.

Revelation 21:10–11: "And he carried me away in the Spirit to a mountain great and high, and showed me the holy city Jerusalem, coming down out of heaven from God, having the glory of God: her light was like unto a stone most precious, as it were a jasper stone, clear as crystal." In some of the very modern versions it says, "her brilliance, her radiance." Perfectly right. We get the word phosphorescence, "light giving, light-bearer" from this.

Verse 18b: "And the city was pure gold, like unto pure glass."

Verse 21b: "And the street of the city was pure gold, as it were transparent glass."

Verse 23: "And the city hath no need of the sun, neither of the moon, to shine upon it: for the glory of God did lighten it." That is its light, its fire, if you like, its flame. There are a number of words used in Scripture for lamp and really one of them should always be translated torch. It is not the kind of torch we use but the old fashioned torch which was dipped in oil and lit, that great roaring thing that gave light. The other is the word used of a lamp which contained oil especially made to go in a stand. Here you have it. "The lamp thereof is the Lamb."

Verse 24 shows us the stand. "And the nations shall walk amidst the light thereof." So you have the stand with the lamp, the Lord Jesus, and the glory of God in the lamp shining out and giving light to everyone. The idea is that this whole city is like a great golden lampstand giving light, revealing divine things, expressing the character of God, showing the heart of God, revealing the mind of God, and proclaiming the Word of God— giving light.

Revelation 22:5: "And there shall be night no more; and they need no light of lamp, neither light of sun; for the Lord God shall give them light: and they shall reign for ever and ever." The Lord God shall give them light.

The Beginning and End of the Book of Revelation

All of that is rather wonderful. What does it mean? It means that the book of Revelation opens and closes with the lampstand all of gold—the testimony of Jesus.

> *... and of the testimony of Jesus Christ*
> *... for the word of God and the testimony of Jesus*
> *Revelation 1:2b, 9b*

> *I Jesus have sent mine angel to testify unto you.*
> *Revelation 22:16*

It is the testimony of Jesus. "To testify unto you these things for the churches." It is not *to* the churches but *for* the churches. The word literally means over the churches, concerning the churches, for the churches. "I am the root and the offspring of David, the bright, the morning star. And the Spirit and the bride say, Come."

> *I testify unto every man that heareth the words of the*
> *prophecy of this book.*
> *Revelation 22:18*

Who is this testifying? It is not John the apostle; it is the Lord. It is the testimony of Jesus. How solemn! How solemn! Everyone who hears the words of the prophecy of this book ... if any man add, if any man take away ...

He who testifieth these things saith, Yea: I come quickly.

Revelation 22:20a

The book of Revelation opens with the seven golden lampstand and the Lord in the midst, and it ends with the one golden lampstand, the Lord Jesus Christ Himself the lamp, the glory of God, the light. It begins with the testimony of Jesus and it ends with the testimony of Jesus. To me it is full of very real significance.

The Spirit and the Bride

I find it extraordinary that we have here in verse 17 this phrase: "The Spirit and the bride say, Come." When we really think about it, it is quite extraordinary, isn't it? If we had heard, "And the Lord says, 'Come,'" it would not be so extraordinary as the Spirit and the bride saying, "Come."

What is it? "I Jesus have sent mine angel to testify unto you these things" over the churches, concerning the churches. "I am the root and the offspring of David," the explanation of the Old Testament. "I am the morning star," that is, the beginning of God's day, the day of God as opposed to the night of man. What next? Before He says anymore about the testimony, suddenly the Spirit breaks in and says, "The Spirit and the bride say, 'Come.'" To whom are they saying it? To the churches. The Spirit and the bride are saying, "Come." Now, take note of all that is written in this book. The Spirit and the bride say, "Come." Let him that will, come—so tender. "He that is athirst, let him

come: he that will, let him take of the water of life freely."
Whatever holds us back? This is the testimony of Jesus.

It is the Spirit and the bride that say, "Come." In other words, this whole matter of the golden lampstand or the testimony of Jesus is all to do with the bride, and the Holy Spirit's energies are bent on the producing, the preparation, and the equipping of that bride. That is why we find that it is the Holy Spirit who introduces the bride. If I may put it reverently but perhaps very untheologically, it is the Holy Spirit who is going to give the bride away. That is the kind of picture you have. It is the wedding and the Spirit says, "Don't be out of this. Don't be denied this. Don't come short of this." The Spirit and the bride say, "Come." He that is athirst let him come. He that will—that's it, isn't it? He that will, let him drink of the water of life. Oh, how we love to blame others when we are not being met, but we can receive it; just go directly to the Lord. He that will, let him come.

The Churches

However, we cannot just stop there. We have got to say something more to do with the testimony of Jesus in conclusion of this matter to do with the testimony of Jesus. It is in fact even more revealing to note that the term churches is used alone throughout the first three chapters of the book of Revelation. You will find no other term except churches, or the church at—"Write this to the church at Ephesus. ... Write this to the church at Smyrna"—and so on.

We have already said that the term churches signifies the church in its practical expression on earth and in time. That is what is in view: the church locally expressed. It is not without vital significance that this term churches never again appears in the whole book of Revelation until it reappears in Revelation 22:16: "I Jesus have sent mine angel to testify unto you these things concerning the churches," or "over the churches." In other words, I think we ought to understand that there is an essential link between the churches and the city of God. Otherwise, why does the Lord come back to it?

First, there is so much in the first three chapters, then absolute silence as far as this term is concerned until we reach the conclusion of everything, and then the last, as it were, epilogue. We are back again to the matter of the churches. Now what is it? The thing that the Holy Spirit tries to underline through this is the link between the church in its practical expression on earth and in time and the eternal church or the city of God, the bride.

To him that overcometh ...
He that overcometh ...
To him that overcometh ...
Revelation 2:7, 11, 17

(This is to all seven churches.)

He that overcometh shall inherit these things; and I will be his
God, and he shall be my son.
Revelation 21:7

Overcoming Linked to the Bride

In other words, overcoming in the context of the churches is linked to being part of the bride. Of course, we all accept that possibly, but in practice it is the hardest thing of all. In other words, it means this: there is no fire escape. There is no way to get out when things get too hot for you. You have got to stay, and you have got to go through, providing the lampstand is there. It is an extraordinary fact that the lampstand is there in spite of all kinds of seaminess, dirt and much else. The Lord in His mercy and grace keeps it there and will not remove it without severe warning. He will not permit anyone to escape. His whole message is to overcome in this. You are not going to get away from it. If you do, you will lose your part in the bride.

Don't you agree with me that this is just the line the devil takes with us? How he inflates things, how he blows up things, how he magnifies things with one great objective, and that is to get us out. We think it is all flesh and blood. We think it is all a question of people being difficult. We think it is all a question of things being wrong. But behind it all is the enemy trying to cancel our place in the city.

Now, once you see this you realise how amazing this book of Revelation is. It is not taking away from the majesty of the vision, the dramatic content of the vision through the book of Revelation to bring it all down to a matter of the church locally. Not at all. Indeed, I can go much further and say that the whole of this book with its tremendous visions of dragons and harlots and beasts and false prophets and other things is all to do with the churches.

Satanic Cunning and Antagonism

In other words, put it like this: Against the background of colossal conflict and upheaval that you find in the book of Revelation all the time—seas heaving, great beasts coming up out of the sea, another beast coming like an earthquake out of the earth, frogs coming up, signs in the heavens, angels, a third of the earth being burnt up, a third of the living things in the sea dying, a third of the green things shriveling up—against that kind of background, you see satanic cunning and antagonism all the way through.

The Dragon

Oh, the hatred of Satan, that dragon, who is waiting for that woman to give birth to the child in order to swallow it up. However, God outwits the devil by catching the man child up to heaven and then the dragon is furious and goes off to make war with the rest of the seed of the woman and those who hold the testimony of Jesus. It is extraordinary, and it is satanic cunning.

The Woman and the Scarlet Beast

Why, you see this scarlet beast and on it a beautiful lady. She is absolutely beautiful—painted, seductive, with beautiful features. She is gilded with pure gold and she has precious stones and pearl on her. It is satanic cunning and antagonism. She is a prostitute. She is not the virgin bride of the Lamb, but the mother of harlots and the abominations of the earth. This is satanic cunning and antagonism.

Antichrist System

As we read this book of Revelation, even if we do not understand it, we see an awful lot in it that speaks of satanic cunning and antagonism all the way through. Against this background of an iron-like, world-wide antichrist system everything that has gone before in the civilisation of man, particularly western civilisation, has been produced. There is a conglomeration of these systems in the whole civilisation going right back to Babylon, Persia, Greece, Rome, and modern democracy, and so on. There emerges this iron-like antichrist system with trade unions that control everyone; stamped identity cards with the mark of the beast, and no one can buy or sell unless they have that identity card. They must starve to death.

The Counterfeit Church

Then, there is a counterfeit church. There are two women in the book of Revelation. One is the bride, the wife of the Lamb, the other is a prostitute. One is New Jerusalem, the other is Babylon. One is the Lamb, the other is a beast, a second beast that looks like a Lamb and speaks like a dragon. It is a world-wide counterfeit church. That is the background.

The Climax of the Battle of the Ages

Against that background is the final ultimate climax of the long battle of the ages going right back to when Lucifer said, "I will be like the Most High," and fell. It goes right back to the Garden of Eden to the moment when man fell. It goes back to when Cain murdered Abel; right the way through the long sordid history of mankind—a tremendous battle.

Oh, how many times Satan has tried to destroy Christ! He has tried to destroy the Messianic line. He has tried to destroy the promised seed of the woman, but he has never ever succeeded. It is the long battle of the ages. Think of it! Think of the days of our Lord Jesus when Herod in fury slew every man child up to the age of two years of age in Bethlehem and the whole surrounding country side. What a battle! What sorrow! What misery! But it was all Satan. People thought it was just some cruel despot, but it was not. Behind it was Satan trying to get at God's Christ. He hates Christ because Christ is the one who will fill the throne of God and Satan said, "I will exalt my throne to the throne of God."

All the way through church history, no matter where it is, when the Christians were murdered, persecuted, wherever it has happened—the dark ages of the church when Satan tried to destroy the light and overcome it and stamp it out until that tremendous outburst of divine life and the lampstand was back— Wycliffe, Hus, Luther, Calvin, and so on. However, here in this book is the final, the climax, and it is called Jacob's Trouble. Now, Jacob has had a lot of trouble; it seems to have been the lot of Jacob to have trouble, but it is called Jacob's Trouble—something such as has never come upon man in the whole history of this world. The Lord Jesus Himself said, "Pray that it may not come upon you." Fancy the Lord saying that to us. Daniel says it will be a time such as has never been, nor ever will be. It is the climax of the battle of the age.

Now, against that the whole progress and ultimate triumph of the testimony of Jesus is set, and it begins with the most mundane, ordinary, routine local churches. Isn't it extraordinary? Only God can do that. If I were writing a book I would say, "We would like to cut out places like that. We must start in some great conference where we have a great gathering of all the Christians together with marvellous singing and wonderful times. That is where we will start, and then we will trace the whole story of the progress of the testimony of Jesus right the way through until finally its triumph in the end." Not the Lord; he brings it all down to little mundane local situations—this church here, that church there, the other church there, and so on.

What is the Lord trying to do? I tell you exactly what the Lord is trying to do. He is putting everything into its right context at the beginning of the book of Revelation. The whole story of the testimony of Jesus, its progress, its ultimate triumph is connected with the church in its practical expression in time and on earth. That means you and me. That's it!

The Connection of the Church to the Testimony of Jesus

The testimony of Jesus is intimately bound up with the churches. If they lose their true character, their true constitution, and their true function, the testimony is gravely compromised, dishonoured and even lost. In other words, the lampstand is removed. Then what happens? It was a mighty movement of God, prophetic in its content, marvellous things happening, significant things happening. In these mundane, ordinary, unworthy, insignificant lives brought together and built together there was a sense of the moving of the Spirit of God, some sense of eternal destiny, some sense of purpose. It all goes and it just becomes meetings, and preaching, and theology, and colleges, and degrees, and positions, and so on. Isn't that church history?

Go back to the Puritans. Go to the library and see some of those books: So and so, minister of the gospel in the church at so and so. Just take the titles—what a moving of the Spirit of God there was! Things happened. Take the Waldensians; sometimes it was known, but hard to believe, that they spoke in tongues and had interpretation. That upset the Roman Catholics to no end. The Anabaptists, that much maligned group, were called extremists and fanatic. Maybe there were some, but there was much also that was of God. It was a moving of God. If we look at the early Methodists, we only have to read Wesley's journal to see some of the things that happened. The testimony was there. People were being changed, transformed. There was the most extraordinary foreordination of events.

What was it? It was the testimony of Jesus. But what happened? Look at church history. Some twenty years after when the lampstand was gone, it is just dead. It has died. It is now a monument to what has happened. It is a kind of gravestone. Here lies the body of Quakerism, born so and so, died so and so. Rest in peace. Or here lies the body of something else, born so and so, died so and so. Rest in peace. What has happened? The lampstand is gone. When the lampstand was there, it was vibrant with life. This is just the situation we face today, and I believe it is the supreme battle of the Spirit of God. The testimony of Jesus—lost.

The situation we face today is just this: the testimony of Jesus is gravely compromised, dishonoured, and lost for the majority, surely the greater part of the golden lampstands have been removed. Where can you go in the earth and feel in your spirit the lampstand is there? There are places, thank God, but when you think of the Christians everywhere, where is the lampstand? What has happened? I say, this is the supreme battle. No wonder the Holy Spirit confronted the prophet Zechariah at a point when everything was in ruins and the building, which was partly started but not finished, was just bits and pieces everywhere. The Lord said to him: "See," and what did he see? A golden lampstand, and what more did he see? Two olive trees pouring gold into it. "Not by might, nor by power, but by my Spirit, saith the Lord of hosts" (4:6b). God is seeking by His Spirit to recover that testimony.

We must never forget, however important the question of personal, spiritual character and growth is, this matter of the testimony of Jesus is more than that. Now, I must make myself clear on this point; I do not want to give the wrong impression. It is true, absolutely true that the Lord is concerned vitally with our personal walk with Him. The very way the Lord speaks to each of those churches reveals that. What does He say? "To him that overcomes," not to those that overcome. He does not speak collectively and say, "All right, those of you who overcome will be in it." He says to him, to her. It is vital, this matter of the personal walk, absolutely vital. The Lord desires truth in the inward parts of our being so that in each of our lives there is a consistency with the testimony that has been entrusted to us. That must be so. Now whatever it is, whether it is spiritual character, whether it is progressive growth in Christ of each one of us personally, whether it is fullness of devotion to Him or personal faithfulness, it is all absolutely foundational. It is absolutely foundational that no one hide in the corporate. Let no one hide in the collective in this matter. It is to him that overcomes.

The Recovery of the Testimony of Jesus

However, let us get this quite, quite clear. Having said that, we must underline the fact that the recovery of the testimony of Jesus is very, very much a question of the recovery of the true character and organic constitution of the church. If you do not understand that, go away and ask the Lord about it. It is essential. People seem to think that the question of the testimony of Jesus is just a matter of a personal walk. It is not! That is foundational and essential. The message is to him that overcomes, but that is not the point. The point really is the recovery of the testimony of Jesus in the true character of the church and its organic constitution. If that cannot be brought into being by the Spirit of God, the lampstand is not there in the first place. How tremendous that is!

All these points we have mentioned in these previous studies are all vital to this question of the testimony of Jesus—the headship of Christ, the heavenliness of Christ, the fellowship of the life of Christ, the fellowship of Christ, the oneness of Christ, the practical local expression of Christ, the manifested presence of Christ. All these things are summed up in the testimony of Jesus: absolute Lordship, all of God, produced out of His life—organic, not organised—the fellowship, one beaten work forged together, all part of Him, the oneness of Christ, who is the oneness, His life, His character, His nature, the local expression.

Where were the seven golden lampstands? Ephesus, Smyrna, Thyatira, Pergamum, Sardis, Philadelphia, Laodicea, that is where they were. That is where Christ has got to be for the testimony of Jesus is brought down to mundane, ordinary terms, but vital terms. Do you talk about loving the saints? God says: how are you getting on with them where you are worshipping, where you are supposed to be gathering together? Do you talk about the unity of Christ? How are you getting on there? It is where it is all brought down to practical, down to earth terms. Of course the manifested presence of Christ is the most essential thing of all. Without it we are nothing. The church is the place where the Lord is seen, where He is known, where He is expressed, where He is understood, where the world can touch Him and He can touch the world. That is us. Or should we put it this way? That is what we should be, and by the grace of God that is what He would like to do with us.

Shall we pray:

Dear Lord, we do pray together that Thou wouldst make real all of this to us. Thou knowest our need, Lord. We are a needy people, but we praise thee, Lord, that thou art with us and thou art ready to take us onward Thyself. We pray that Thou wouldst make each one of us true overcomers because of Thyself. Thou hast bidden us to come. Thou hast said, "Any that are athirst let them come to Thee." Oh, Lord, we pray that we might be those who really know what it is to come to Thee and drink of Thee. Hear us, Lord, as together we place all this into Thy hands. We commit one another into Thy hands and into Thy keeping and pray, beloved Lord, that Thou wouldst make us those who in our hearts really understand what that testimony is and those who hold it. We ask it in the name of our Lord Jesus Christ. Amen.

6.
The Recovery of the Testimony of Jesus

Genesis 12:7–8

And the Lord appeared unto Abram, and said, Unto thy seed will I give this land: and there builded he an altar unto the Lord, who appeared unto him. And he removed from thence unto the mountain on the east of Beth-el, and pitched his tent, having Beth-el on the west, and Ai on the east: and there he builded an altar unto the Lord, and called upon the name of the Lord.

Genesis 35:1–3

And God said unto Jacob, Arise, go up to Beth-el, and dwell there: and make there an altar unto God, who appeared unto thee when thou fleddest from the face of Esau thy brother. Then Jacob said unto his household, and to all that were with him, Put away the foreign gods that are among you, and purify yourselves, and change your garments: and let us arise, and go up to Beth-el; and I will make

there an altar unto God, who answered me in the day of my distress,
and was with me in the way which I went.

Genesis 28:11–17

And he [Jacob] lighted upon a certain place, and tarried there all
night, because the sun was set; and he took one of the stones of the
place, and put it under his head, and lay down in that place to sleep.
And he dreamed; and, behold, a ladder set up on the earth, and the
top of it reached to heaven; and, behold, the angels of God ascending
and descending on it. And, behold, the Lord stood above it, and said,
I am the Lord, the God of Abraham thy father, and the God of Isaac:
the land whereon thou liest, to thee will I give it, and to thy seed;
and thy seed shall be as the dust of the earth, and thou shalt spread
abroad to the west, and to the east, and to the north, and to the
south: and in thee and in thy seed shall all the families of the earth be
blessed. And, behold, I am with thee, and will keep thee whithersoever
thou goest, and will bring thee again into this land; for I will not leave
thee, until I have done that which I have spoken to thee of. And Jacob
awaked out of his sleep, and he said, Surely the Lord is in this place;
and I knew it not. And he was afraid, and said, How dreadful is this
place! This is none other than the house of God, and this is the gate
of heaven.

(That of course was Beth-el.)

Genesis 28:19

And he called the name of that place Beth-el:
(house of God)

Genesis 22:1–2

And it came to pass after these things, that God did prove Abraham, and said unto him, Abraham; and he said, Here am I. And he said, Take now thy son, thine only son, whom thou lovest, even Isaac, and get thee into the land of Moriah; and offer him there for a burnt-offering upon one of the mountains which I will tell thee of ... And they came to the place which God had told him of; and Abraham built the altar there, and laid the wood in order, and bound Isaac his son, and laid him on the altar, upon the wood. And Abraham stretched forth his hand, and took the knife to slay his son. And the angel of the Lord called unto him out of heaven, and said, Abraham, Abraham: and he said, Here am I. And he said, Lay not thy hand upon the lad, neither do thou anything unto him; for now I know that thou fearest God, seeing thou hast not withheld thy son, thine only son, from me. And Abraham lifted up his eyes, and looked, and, behold, behind him a ram caught in the thicket by his horns: and Abraham went and took the ram, and offered him up for a burnt-offering in the stead of his son. And Abraham called the name of that place Jehovah-jireh: as it is said to this day, In the mount of the Lord it shall be provided. (That was Mount Moriah.)

1 Chronicles 21:15–16, 27

And God sent an angel unto Jerusalem to destroy it: and as he was about to destroy, the Lord beheld, and he repented him of the evil, and said to the destroying angel, It is enough; now stay thy hand. And the angel of the Lord was standing by the threshing-floor of Ornan the Jebusite. And David lifted up his eyes, and saw the angel

of the Lord standing between earth and heaven, having a drawn
sword in his hand stretched out over Jerusalem. Then David and
the elders, clothed in sackcloth, fell upon their faces ... And the Lord
commanded the angel; and he put up his sword again into the sheath
thereof.

I Chronicles 22:1
Then David said, This is the house of the Lord God, and this is the
altar of burnt-offering for Israel.
(That was Mount Moriah again.)

II Chronicles 3:1
Then Solomon began to build the house of the Lord at Jerusalem
on mount Moriah, where the Lord appeared unto David his father,
which he made ready in the place that David had appointed, in the
threshing-floor of Ornan the Jebusite.

Exodus 40:6–7
And thou shalt set the altar of burnt-offering before the door of the
tabernacle of the tent of meeting. And thou shalt set the laver between
the tent of meeting and the altar, and shalt put water therein.
(Everything is to do with an altar and the house.)

Ezra 3:1–3, 6, 8–13
And when the seventh month was come, and the children of Israel
were in the cities, the people gathered themselves together as one
man to Jerusalem. Then stood up Jeshua the son of Jozadak, and his

brethren the priests, and Zerubbabel the son of Shealtiel, and his brethren, and builded the altar of the God of Israel, to offer burnt-offerings thereon, as it is written in the law of Moses the man of God. And they set the altar upon its base; for fear was upon them because of the peoples of the countries: and they offered burnt-offerings thereon unto the Lord, even burnt-offerings morning and evening ... From the first day of the seventh month began they to offer burnt-offerings unto the Lord: but the foundation of the temple of the Lord was not yet laid...Now in the second year of their coming unto the house of God at Jerusalem, in the second month, began Zerubbabel the son of Shealtiel, and Jeshua the son of Jozadak, and the rest of their brethren the priests and the Levites, and all they that were come out of the captivity unto Jerusalem, and appointed the Levites, from twenty years old and upward, to have the oversight of the work of the house of the Lord. Then stood Jeshua with his sons and his brethren, Kadmiel and his sons, the sons of Judah, together, to have the oversight of the workmen in the house of God: the sons of Henadad, with their sons and their brethren the Levites. And when the builders laid the foundation of the temple of the Lord, they set the priests in their apparel with trumpets, and the Levites the sons of Asaph with cymbals, to praise the Lord, after the order of David king of Israel. And they sang one to another in praising and giving thanks unto the Lord, saying, For he is good, for his lovingkindness endureth for ever toward Israel. And all the people shouted with a great shout, when they praised the Lord, because the foundation of the house of the Lord was laid. But many of the priests and Levites and heads of fathers' houses, the old men that had seen the first house, when the *foundation of this house was laid before their eyes, wept with a loud voice; and many shouted aloud for joy: so that the people could not discern the noise of the shout of joy from the noise of the weeping of the people; for the people shouted with a loud shout, and the noise was heard afar off.*

Ezekiel 40:47
And he measured the court, a hundred cubits long, and a hundred cubits broad, foursquare; and the altar was before the house.

Ezekiel 47:1
And he brought me back unto the door of the house; and, behold, waters issued out from under the threshold of the house eastward (for the forefront of the house was toward the east); and the waters came down from under, from the right side of the house, on the south of the altar.

(This great river of life came from inside the house from the altar and flowed out through the city into the whole land so that everything was changed by this great river.)

We come now to the conclusion of these studies on why we are at Halford House. We have said a lot, yet in answering this question we have still not touched on the real key to everything. We have said that the headship of Christ is vital, the church's body is a heavenly thing which is something out of heaven in a different order altogether to anything down here. We have said that the church is an organism and not an organisation, that the church is the fellowship of Christ, and so on. But we have still not actually touched on the key to this whole matter. We have answered the question but the point is how does it all come to pass? We can go to theological courses, we can go to Bible colleges, we can come here on a poorer level and learn something about the church or some other matter, but the fact remains that in the end the practical question is: How? Not only why, but how? We may have given a good explanation and a good answer to our question: Why am I at Halford House? We may have satisfied ourselves about it all, but we must be very careful that in answering our question accurately and soundly and scripturally, we may still be in a fool's paradise. The *how* in the end is the almighty question or if you like, it is the million dollar question. *How* can we see the church recovered in a practical expression? *How* can we see the testimony of Jesus that we have been considering over the last few weeks recovered and restored? *How* can we see God really moving in such a way as to express Himself in terms that are found in the New Testament? What is the secret, the key to the source of the life of God in which everything lies inherent?

The Cross and the Spirit

The key is two-fold: it is the cross and the Spirit. When we say the cross and the Spirit, in that one simple sentence we have encompassed the whole of the New Testament. Indeed, I can go further and say we have encompassed the whole of the Bible. But how? The answer is in that one simple statement, the cross and the Spirit; not the cross alone nor the Spirit alone, but the cross and the Spirit. The church, as the body of Christ, is a spiritual organism. It may have a tremendous amount of organisation, but it is the original source of its organisation that counts. It is an organism and its organisation develops from the life of God that is within it. As we have seen in our studies, it cannot be put together by man. It cannot be set up by man. People talk about "my church," "my people," "my prayer meetings." Ministers often talk about this, especially about "my pulpit," and so on. But it is quite foreign to the New Testament. The apostle Paul, who perhaps more than anyone else, might have felt a claim to talk about "my churches" never refers to them as such or "my people" in that sense. It cannot be put together by man.

The Old Man has to be Removed

I remember a young man coming a while ago and asking us about how we run the place. We asked him what he was, and he said he was the same as us; he ran two or three churches. That simple statement gave everything away. There was no need to say another word.

Indeed, I think we have to say that not only is the church a spiritual organism and cannot be put together or set up by man but, and this is tremendously important, the Holy Spirit has to reveal it to our hearts and not just to our heads. Man, as he is, has got to be removed entirely by the work of the Holy Spirit through the cross, and he has to be thoroughly dealt with. Far from putting people into some kind of Bible college just to refine what is in them naturally, the Holy Spirit's work is to destroy and break up what is in us naturally, to remove altogether what we are so that what we are can be used; that is the paradox.

The apostle Paul is broken up in the death, completely broken up, yet in the end the Holy Spirit used his mind in an unparalleled way. Paul's mind could not have been used with all its native wit and intelligence, its native genius. However, when it was broken, when he was removed and broken up, then the Spirit of God could fall upon him and use him.

How different this is from much of our modern methods in training one another. The idea is: "You have this capacity or that ability. Come on and concecrate it to the service of God, dedicate it to His service." Of course, the tragic results are seen in the church where we have man's work instead of the Spirit's work and make it appear to be God's work, but it is not; it is wood, hay and stubble. The wood, hay and stubble, though perhaps gilded, are of man's own nature and not the gold or the silver or the precious stone of the nature and character of Christ. Before the church can be expressed in the simplest way, the Holy Spirit has to remove man which is you and me as we are. That is the crux of the problem. Make no mistake about it. The crux of the problem is not getting people interested in this matter of the church, or not getting people to meet together, though I must say that the flesh finds it tiresome after a while. After a few years it has become used to it all and strains to get a way out of it and find something new and novel. Believe me there is no problem in getting people together. The problem is to get people to present their bodies as a living sacrifice to God, which God can then break open, the Holy Spirit can fall upon, and really use. I say one life like that is worth a million.

You can have conference after conference after conference, you can have missionary society after missionary society, you can study the works of Christian workers, but to have one man like the apostle Paul, one man like Timothy, one man that is devoted to God in such a way that he can be broken open and used is worth all the rest put together.

Never before in the history of the church have we had as much money as we now have, strangely enough, in spite of all the appeals received on every side. We have never had as much accumulated money in Christian hands as today nor have we ever had so many councils, committees, and boards cluttered up with titles and wealthy people, moneyed people. Never in the whole history of the church have we ever had so many Christian workers. Did you know that? Never have we had the media that we have today—the printed page, recordings, television, radio, means not only of communication but of transport which brings the whole world into a small area that can be easily encompassed. We have never had anything like it before, and yet we are losing the battle. You only have to open any missionary magazine, read any survey or statistic, and everyone will tell you that we are losing the battle in spite of the population explosion and much else.

The Difference between the Early Church and the Modern-Day Church

What is the difference between us and the early church? There were one hundred and twenty unlettered, untaught people. They had not been to a university; there were no councils, no committees or boards cluttered up with titled people or moneyed people. There was nothing of the kind. There were not any Bible colleges, theological courses or anything else. They did not even possess the principal of a theological seminary among the hundred and twenty. Yet that hundred and twenty were destined to turn Jerusalem upside down, and indeed to turn the Roman Empire upside down. Comparatively speaking, they took the gospel over the whole world. Within a hundred years of the death of the Lord Jesus Christ there was a church in India, a church in China, and a church in these British islands. It is an incredible story. The secret to it all was that they knew something of the cross and the Spirit.

The church knows, after all, no uncrucified man. There is no such thing as an uncrucified Christian. Every single man or woman who has been saved and placed in Christ is crucified. That is inherent within their salvation. It is not a Christian trying to crucify himself, but you and I are crucified and that is a fact. There is no argument; it is a fact. You may not be in the experience of it, but it is a fact. Why is this so? Who was crucified? Not you; Jesus Christ was crucified and God took you into Jesus Christ when He was crucified two thousand years ago. Therefore, there is not one single person by the grace of God and the foreordination of God who is in Christ Jesus that has not been crucified. Whether you have entered into it or not, the fact inherent within your spiritual birth is your crucifixion. That is the fact; that is what baptism is about. The church knows no such thing as an uncrucified person. We are all crucified with Christ, and thank God we were all buried with Him, and more than that we are all made alive together with Him. We are in Him; He is the new Man risen from the dead, the firstborn from the dead, and the firstborn among many brothers. This is the whole meaning of the church. Furthermore, we are not only alive in Him, but we are living members of Him. We are the fellowship of Christ, living members, living parts of Him and of one another. The whole nature of this thing is so amazing.

Of course, I do understand that is the fact; but have we entered into it? That is the point. Have we entered into it? We can only enter into it by the cross and the Spirit. So it is the measure in which we possess what is ours in Christ that will be the measure in which we know this experience. The measure in which we are prepared to allow the cross to work in our lives will be the measure in which the Holy Spirit is able to bring us in. So take great note of this word.

The Church is within the Life of Christ

The church, the house of God, all that we have talked about lies inherent within the resurrection life of Jesus Christ. Can I put it this way? It is the very life of Jesus Christ born at Nazareth, tested through thirty-three years, anointed by the Holy Spirit when He was baptised in the river Jordan, tempted of the devil, transfigured in glory, coming down finally to go through to the cross and into the grave and out on the other side. That is the life that is in you and me; it is no different. It is not that we have another degree of life, another kind of life, another type of life, that when the Lord Jesus died, suddenly another kind of life came into existence. Not at all! Remember the words of the Lord Jesus: "Oh, how I am straitened" (see Luke 12:49). The life was in Him but He could not give it out. There they all were, unleavened, salty, failing disciples. He wanted to give them Himself; He wanted to get into them, don't you see? He could see that they could do nothing else but fail. They were learning it all in their mind, but what a mess they got into. How quickly they could deny what they had learned in their mind just like you and me. We can come to Bible study after Bible study on a Thursday evening, we can get it all up here and blame the preacher, poor thing, as if he is able to get into you. He cannot get into you anymore than anyone else can. The fact of the matter is we can learn and learn and learn, but until the cross came as a fact, there was no possibility of that life getting into us. But when the cross came, the life was made available to us. That is the secret of the cross and the Spirit.

In other words, many of us live in a kind of pre-Calvary Christian experience. We are walking around with Jesus listening to His words, watching His acts, being excited by His miracles and all the time watching this. Oh, if we could only have a sign, if we could only have this or that, and we are following, following, following, but the thing is not us. It is not in us, and the reason it is not in us is because we are not prepared for the cross. It is inherent within the resurrection life of the Lord Jesus Christ. These seven points we have considered are in fact all the evidence of the life of God, the Spirit of life, unchecked and unhindered in His people. When the life of God is unchecked and unhindered, when the Spirit of life can move freely, then these seven things are immediately expressed; you cannot help it. That is the unfailing way in which you and I can test things amongst the people of God.

Calvary Produced Pentecost

The key to that life is the cross, but we don't always like this key. People speak of it as being heavy. I do not think there is anything very light about the bloodiness of the cross. After all it was a gibbet, a scaffold. What did you expect it to be? Something light? Something you can dance about? Of course not! The cross is a scaffold; it is a guillotine; it is a place of death. How much easier it would be for us if we did not have to go that way, if we could jump into Pentecost without Calvary, if we could get all the glory and all the excitement and all the fullness of Pentecost without the scaffold, without the stench of blood, without the smoke and smell of burnt flesh. It would be wonderful if we could get into Pentecost without the cross, and that is why there is so much counterfeit experience and strange fire because people want to avoid it. They do not want to pay the price, face the facts, face reality. They do not want to face themselves. They want to jump into Pentecost without Calvary. It cannot be done! The cross is the secret of the birth, the growth and the expression of the church. It has ever been the only way to the house of God.

If we go right back to the beginning, we find Abraham building an altar. Where does he build the altar? Between Ai, which means a heap or a ruin, and Bethel, the house of God. He has the ruin of his old nature and self behind him and he has the house of God in front of him, and between it was the altar.

So many people want to try and make the ruin the house. God will not have it. *He will not have it!* This is God's argument with His people all the way through the centuries. He just will not have it. We see it all the way through the different scriptures. What about dear Jacob? What does he see? He sees a vision with a ladder going up into heaven. Most people think of it as a lovely picture. But do you know what it is? There were angels going up and coming down; they were not coming down and going up, but they were going up and coming down. What is it? It is a picture of the house of God, and the Lord standing above it sort of midway between heaven and earth, the means of communication—union and communion.

Jacob may have been a twister, a deceiver and a supplanter, but he saw the point. He was spiritually shrewd. He said, "My goodness, this is none other than the house of God, the gate to heaven." Being an honest man, he also said, "How fearful is this place!" (see Genesis 28:17) Once we begin to see what the house of God is, it is a fearful place to our flesh. Later on in Hebrews it says, "Jacob worshipped at the end of his life" (see 11:21). It was the fear of God but the right kind. His flesh had been dealt with, so he was a worshipper. Worshippers are never critics or murmurers. We can always tell the flesh by the children of Israel because they continually murmured against the Lord; that is the flesh. Worship is a sign of the Spirit.

Let's take Abraham. God told him to take his only son and offer him up. He goes up to a mountain called Mount Moriah and there he offered Isaac. Suddenly the Lord appeared; his son is saved and a ram is offered in his place on the altar. Later on, that very place was to become the site of the altar of burnt offering in the house of the Lord, the temple, that very place which you can see today. That very place became the spot for the house of God.

In Exodus it says, "See that you put the altar in front of the tabernacle" (see 40:29). In other words, if we were all Israelites, if we went through the door there was a big courtyard; the actual size of the tabernacle was quite large. As you go through the outer gate, just inside you will see a great altar. It blocks everything; it obscures everything. Before you can get to the tent of meeting, before you can get to the tabernacle, before you can get to the house of God, the altar blocks the way. When you come to the altar and have accepted all that the altar means, you see a laver, and it is the laver of regeneration. It is the washing of the Word. In other words, one thing is the removing of man, the other thing is birthed from above. One thing is the dealing with what we are naturally, the other is a new nature and a new life from God. One is earth, the other is heaven. So before we can get into the house of God, before we can even get into the church, as it were, before you can see it and know all the wonderful and blessed ministries of the church—the showbread table, the golden altar of incense, the lampstand all of gold—the first thing is the altar and the second thing is the laver. One is negative, the other is positive. One clears the ground, the other brings in what is of God. You cannot get away from it.

When they rebuilt the temple in the days of Zerubbabel, Ezra, and Nehemiah, the first thing they did was to set up the altar. Why, you would say, "Don't be silly. The first thing is to lay the foundation, get the walls up, put the roof on, and then we can have the altar. You cannot offer up things on the altar until we have the place done, can we?"

But no, the Lord says the first thing is the altar, the second thing is the foundation, and the third thing is the building. How full of spiritual principle it is! God starts with the cross. Once the altar is in its place, the Holy Spirit comes in and the work on the foundation begins and the building goes up. The whole book of Haggai and Zechariah are woven into that.

If you go to Ezekiel's great vision in chapter 43, we find the same thing again. Then there is a great altar right in front of the house. Then when he has seen everything that is so marvellous about this new house, this new temple that is going to be built, he is taken back and he sees a great river beginning like a little trickle. There is a little tiny bubbling stream coming from the altar. Where is the altar? It is in the house of God before the gate of the house of God. There it is bubbling up. That little stream becomes an Amazon-like river that changes everything by its fertility and life-giving power. It is all from the altar—no altar, no river.

Calvary produced Pentecost. Pentecost did not produce Calvary. *Calvary* produced Pentecost. No matter where you look you will find it. In Ephesians and elsewhere it speaks of the Calvary side of it, the blood of the Lamb, the blood of Christ. Then suddenly it speaks of the works of the Spirit—in one Spirit. Then it speaks of being built together, growing into a holy temple in the Lord.

The Seed Falls into the Ground and Dies

The Lord Jesus said, "Destroy this temple, and in three days I will raise it up" (John 2:19). He spake of His body. Of course, we know that. The greatest example of it is when the Greeks came (who were Gentiles) to see Jesus. They were not even God-fearers; they were absolute Gentiles. They came to Philip and said, "We would see Jesus" (see John 12:21). Of course, they were fearful; they thought that the Lord being a Jew would not have anything to do with Gentiles because of the ceremonial uncleanness. They went to Philip, who had a Greek name, and said to him: "Sir, we would like to see Jesus." Philip went to Andrew and they both went to Jesus and told Him. The Lord

Jesus said to them these wonderful words: "Verily, verily, I say unto you, Except a grain of wheat fall into the ground and die, it abideth by itself alone; but if it die, it beareth much fruit" (John 12:24). Jesus died, and His death has borne much fruit. Isn't that a rather extraordinary way of answering a quite simple, straight forward question? We would like to see the Lord. Then we get all this talk about falling into the ground and dying. What is it about? Surely He could have said, "No, I am too busy," or He could have said, "Yes, I will give them two minutes." Why did He say what He did? It is this whole matter again. The Lord Jesus said, "Wait, wait, wait. They can come and see Me, they can come and talk with Me, but they will not get anything. They will only know Me after the flesh. Just wait; when I have fallen into the ground and died, there will be thousands of Greeks in My body; and not only Greeks but Gentiles from all over the world will come and become fellow members of the body when I've fallen into the ground and died."

If you go on in that passage in John you will find the Lord spoke of His death saying, "And I, if I be lifted up from the earth, will draw all men unto myself" (12:32). How could it not be clear to us? It is the cross, and then the Spirit draws us. I have said Calvary precedes Pentecost and it is not only historical but also in our collective and individual experience. We cannot come into any real understanding and experience of the church until we have first come into a real experience of the cross.

If you feel out of it, do not blame others. We all get into this terrible fault of murmuring just like the children of Israel in the wilderness. It is always so-and-so or so-and-so, and the Lord hears every word. He knows where there is dishonesty and He knows where we are causing trouble. We have to be done with that. It is better to own up to it and say, "I am in the fault in this matter." There may be faults in others, but the fact of the matter is that if the Lord can get His way in me there could be a great change. This matter of the cross is so tremendous. We say we feel out of it, we feel excluded, we feel this, we feel that. It is amazing what happens. Sometimes some people feel messages are just *aimed* at them. The most extraordinary thing is that sometimes people come to us and say, "It is *aimed* at me!" To tell the honest truth I had not even known this person was there, but you do not dare say it. If I were to say "I did not even notice you" that would be the end! Any of you who have done any speaking know as well as I do that sometimes you do not notice people at all. There is no disrespect, you are only conscious of the message that God has given you and you give it. This kind of thing is so amazing! People say, "They *all* feel so and so." Again and again we have heard this kind of thing. We say to them, "They *all* feel so and so? Have you asked them?" They say, "No. I know it! They are all so narrow."

There are many examples of this kind of thing. We could spend the whole evening going into a rather humorous vein because really and truly it is rather funny when it comes down to it. The fact is that we have only ourselves to blame if we do not really come into it. People say, "They are so unfriendly." But lo and behold, this dear person never does a thing, doesn't even say 'boo' to a ghost. They expect everyone to come to them instead of going out and doing something, just simple little things. The root of the whole thing is this: we, I, you must first come into a real understanding of the experience of the cross if we are going to know the church.

The Tragic Result of Bypassing the Cross

There are just a few things I would like you to note. The first is that in the light of this we will sum up all these studies. The tragic result of bypassing the cross and setting up the church can be seen only too clearly in the complex situation which we believers face today. Why, look at it! Do you honestly believe that all these "isms" and "ites" and everything else that goes by the name of the church are really God's mind? Isn't it rather extraordinary that they all claim to be built on the pattern of the New Testament? No wonder the agnostic says, "Does God know His own mind?" When we have complete opposites claiming fervently to be built on the pattern in the New Testament, what a complex situation. What has gone wrong? Why has that organic something not come into being? Or again, why is it that we have had around us everywhere in Europe and in America—I think in America more so than here, not so much the age-old traditions, but oh my, all the encrusted denominations under the sun—once great works of the Spirit of God. What has happened to them? A work that began in the Spirit has ended in the flesh, and everywhere there are the monuments to be viewed. It is a complex situation, isn't it?

There are many groups that claim to be really "New Testament" and have left everything to start again, and what do we find? We find soundness, but deadness, a stultifying organisationalism as great as anything that has been left. That is the complex situation that has resulted from bypassing the cross. The cross would cut that out in its entirety. Why, it would smash the thing at its roots by striking at the source, which is man so that the Spirit might come in.

It would strike at the source that keeps it going, a misguided loyalty to things rather than to Christ.

The Result of the Church Losing Its Practical Expression

The second observation I would like to make is that the absence of the church in practical expression causes all the gifts, the functions and the ministries to lose the greater part of their meaning and purpose. It also means the dissipation of spiritual values. For the most part they are so often not conserved.

Take Billy Graham's crusade as a good example of what I mean. It is a tremendous evangelistic crusade and wouldn't it be glorious if the church were in its right place, and everywhere all over Britain you could see it? Of course, there would be those who would go back. The Scripture itself tells us there will be those who fall by the way. Demas loved the present world (II Timothy 4:10), and you cannot stop that. It is as old as Adam. People have always loved the world and put the world before Christ and gone back. I am sorry to say it, but it is a fact. You cannot stop it. You will always get some spurious conversions; you will always get some superficial conversions. They are not necessarily spurious, but they do not go deep enough. Don't you agree with me that the absence of the church in practical expression means that so many of the gifts, the teaching, the prophetic ministry, many other ministries, and many of the gifts that are in each one of us, for the most part lose their place?

Knowledge of Doctrine and Practical Expression

The third thing I would like to make as an observation is that: the knowledge of the doctrine of the church, though sound, accurate and even full, does not bring it into practical expression. We all know groups that have it absolutely tied up in their head. They could give you a clear definition of the church and everything else, and they do not know the first thing about it in practical experience. That is because no amount of knowledge necessarily means that the church is there, nor does any amount of trying. Oh, have we not all met people trying to build the church, desperately wanting the church to come into being.

The Church in the Life of Christ—Not His Death

My fourth thought is this and I will spend a little longer on this one. The church lies inherent within the life of Christ. That life is made available by the Spirit. It is not in His death. His death was the judgment of God upon our sin. It was the propitiation by Christ for our sin. That death spelled redemption for us, the forgiveness of our sins. We are justified through His death. We have an eternal and legal standing with God through His death, and further, that death means the removing of fallen man altogether, the clearing, if you like, of the ground for God. That is what the cross means. The death of Christ has cleared the ground of you and me. Hallelujah! We are gone. God says, "Out with you! The first thing I will do is save you, and the second thing I will do is remove you!"

We can talk about the cross, but do we understand the burial? The dead person is buried out of sight; the body is gone. God says, "I have saved you to remove you." Now anyone who is unsaved is not removed. They are very much there in the sight of God in all their ugliness, in all their sin, in all their iniquity, in the abomination of their iniquity. They are there in the very sight of God blatantly to be seen. But you and I have been saved and removed. Blessed be His name!

The church is not in His death; the church may have been produced by His death, but it is not in His death. The church is in the life of Christ. If that life will develop, expand and grow, the result will be the house of God. You cannot stop it. If that life can get into two or three believers on the same foundation in Christ in the same place, living together, then once that life starts to flow it will result in the house of God. You cannot stop it. It is the new man. The new man is not the dead man but is the one who is alive from the dead. Everything is in the life of Christ. So it is not knowledge or trying that counts. That can end in a substitute for the real thing. I can get it all up here in my head, be saved, and then try to produce it. The more I try, the more I can put it all together according to the plan, and the more organising ability, the more capability I have in the things of God, the more possibility there is of such a thing resulting. This is what it means when every man's work will be tried so as by fire. Every one of us, whatever we have done is all going to be tried by fire. Not one of us is going to escape. We are all going to be called in, and the fire will try us. What comes through is what is of God; not what appears to be of God, but what is of God will come through and whatever is of myself will be out.

Life Made Available by the Holy Spirit

It is an ever increasing experience of His life individually and corporately that counts—not knowledge but experience. Furthermore, and this is very, very important; it is the Holy Spirit alone who can bring the resurrection life of Christ into us and express it through us initially and progressively. No one else can do it (see Romans 8). It is impossible. It is the Spirit of Him who raised up Christ Jesus from the dead dwelling in us. Then what happens? By the Spirit we put to death the deeds of the body, *we* put to death the deeds of the body, not all the time looking to be delivered from it. We have to do something by the Spirit. Then what happens? We are joint-heirs with Christ, by the Spirit of adoption. It is the body.

Ephesians 1:19a,20a: "And what the exceeding greatness of his power to us-ward who believe, when he raised Jesus Christ from the dead." It is the Spirit again. The Lord Jesus was raised by the Spirit of God. "He gave him to be head over all things to the church which is his body, the fullness of him that filleth all in all" (v. 22, 23). Everything is under His feet; He is Head over all things, and we are the body. It is glorious.

Zechariah had a great vision of a lampstand all of gold (see chapter 4), and he was very concerned about the two olive trees on either side and the olive branches. Why was he bothered about that? Zechariah is like us; he wanted to see where we come into the picture, and the Lord said, "Zechariah, shut up. I do not want where you are to come into the picture." All of you have said, "What is the olive tree, Lord? What are the two olive branches, Lord?" Of course, Zechariah had some inkling. We have all have intuition.

He thought, "I'm quite sure I know what that is. Trees stand for men in the Scriptures, one on either side. Oh, I wonder who they are? Will He say, 'One is Zerubbabel and the other is Joshua?' Will He say, 'One is Zechariah and the other Haggai?'"

The angel of the Lord said, "No, no, no. It is not where *you* come into the picture: it is where I come into the picture." God said, "Zechariah, what do you see? You see a lampstand; that is Me." Then he talks about rebuilding. "That is what I get." Then he comes back to the branches. "Do you know what they are doing? They are emptying gold out of themselves–the material for what I am getting," said the Lord. It is a quite different basis.

We cannot overestimate the fact that it is impossible to know the life of Christ apart from the Holy Spirit. Through the finished work of Christ at Calvary the Holy Spirit is able to make the life of Jesus Christ–eternal life, the very life of God Himself–available to every saved sinner. It does not matter who you are. We are saved sinners. The life of Jesus Christ is made available to us by the Holy Spirit. You cannot know it apart from the Holy Spirit. You can only know your own life, but it will leave you empty and neurotic. But if you know the life of Christ, you will be carried sometimes into the third heaven and hear things perhaps unspeakable, that are not even lawful to utter. That will be the sign of it; you will shut up instead of running around talking, talking, talking, exposing yourself and others. It is something of God.

When the Holy Spirit really works, it is a tremendous thing. There is nothing more wonderful than to know the Holy Spirit. He was the One who brought light out of darkness. He was the One who brought form out of emptiness. He was the One through whom man was created in the image of the Lord Jesus Christ. It is the Holy Spirit who has watched over the purpose of God from the beginning of time until now. It is the Holy Spirit who brought to birth our Lord Jesus Christ having already inspired the prophets at all different phases in the history of God's covenant people. It was the Holy Spirit who fell upon the Lord Jesus Christ at His baptism and anointed Him. It was the Holy Spirit through whom He was transfigured in glory on Mount Tabor. It was the Holy Spirit who enabled Him to offer Himself up on the cross for us all. It was the Holy Spirit who brought again our Lord Jesus, that great Shepherd of the sheep, from the dead. Then, it was when the Lord Jesus ascended to the right hand of God the Father that He received for sinful men and women like you and me, saved by the grace of Jesus Christ, the grace of God He received the promise of that Holy Spirit, God the Spirit, and poured Him forth. That is Pentecost.

The Gifts and the Character of the Head

My dear friends, you have an altogether poor idea of Pentecost if your idea of Pentecost is just and only a little flame of fire, a little bit of fullness, jumping up and being able to preach. Is that your idea of Pentecost? You need to revise it. God's idea of Pentecost is nothing less than this—God the Spirit fell upon saved human beings. In other words, none of us know the fulness of it; if only we did! If only our poor eyes could be opened to see what happened at Pentecost, if only somehow by faith we could claim what has happened for us all at Pentecost. It was the making available of the life of Jesus Christ to every saved sinner by joining them to the one Christ in one body. By that one Spirit making real in them and through them the authority and power of the Head, the gifts of the Head. Then He ascended on high and gave gifts unto men. There is a gift for every one of us because we are joined to the Head who has given the gifts. It does not matter what it is, it is there. Take it. It is in you by the Holy Spirit; it is there. The gifts and the ministries of the Head are given to the members of the body of Christ, but it is the Head that counts. He has given it.

More than that, He is making available to us the character of the Head. Oh, that is more than gifts! You can have a thousand gifts, but one day it will mean nothing. What you need is the character of the Lamb and that is where we all fall short. We all know what it is to have a gift. You can judge me a thousand times on gifts. You can have a gift, but if the character is lacking, the gift is marred. Even if I am a good "coverer-up" and get away with it there would come a day when the character would be seen for what it is. That is what the apostle Paul said, "Having preached to others, I myself might be a reject (I Corinthians 9:27)."

It is tremendous, isn't it? He makes the very presence of the Head real in that body, and now that is the meaning of Pentecost. Don't you see it? Don't you see what happened on the day of Pentecost? Do you really think all that happened was a few people, one-hundred-and-twenty, spoke in tongues and everyone got excited and said, "Oh, they're drunk!" Is that Pentecost? Never! Pentecost was this, and I will die on this issue. That moment the Lord Jesus, who had been straitened in Himself in one human body, suddenly became one hundred and twenty human bodies with the possibility of infinite multiplication. Suddenly–this is the book of Acts, the authority and power of the Lord Jesus, crucified and raised by God, is once again walking on the earth. Listen to them: "By what name have you done these things?" asked the government. "In the name of Jesus Christ of Nazareth whom you slew and God raised up." It is the authority of God.

In one place a few handkerchiefs were taken from the apostle Paul and sent to people and they were healed. Even the Lord Jesus did not do that. He said, "Even greater things you shall do." It is the book of Acts. Do you see what I mean? It is character. Look at Stephen with the face of an angel! Even the Lord Jesus stood up to receive him, he was so beautiful. What happened? Those poor people, were they religious fanatics? No, something had happened! That is what we mean by the church.

What can we say? All these seven points are bound up here. Wouldn't you like to know the Holy Spirit like that? I would. I'm not interested in all this other business. My dear friends, a lot of it is kindergarten nonsense. If you want it, go and have it. However, let me tell you this: if you want what He wants, you are in for something. You are in for it because it is the cross. The Holy Spirit in all His glorious power and infinite fullness refuses to fall on anyone until the cross is there. Oh, He will give you experiences, He will give you blessings, all kinds of things. He will even give you gifts, but He will refuse to do any building work for the city. Nothing is going to get into that city which has not gone the same way as its Master, and that is Calvary. Do you not think, dear child of God, that is right? I do. I will tell you why I think it is right. It would be much nicer if I could say to you like some say, "Now then you can just jump into it; just like that." I say it is nonsense. The Lord has never allowed anything to get into the house which has not gone by way of the altar. Never! Do not think you are an exception. None of us are exceptions to that, none of us at all. If you want to be used of God, if you want what you have in you to be eternal, if you want to find in the end the city, you have to go to the cross. Don't you think that is right? I do. This is the reason why: it requires faith.

If I could just take a great jump and have a glorious excitement and then feel marvellous, there is no faith in it; it is feeling. But if I come up against the scaffold with all the blood, with all the smoke, with all the slaughter, and God says to me, "This is the way. You come here, you go this way and you will know glory." That requires faith. I shrink back, "Oh no, Lord, not that." That is what Jesus did. Oh, surely there is some other way. But there is no other way. You have to go that way if you really would know the Spirit of God. I am sorry. Let me be absolutely clear. It says in the Book that everyone who goes that way shall know a committing of God to them such as others will never know both now and in eternity. At the end you will find it all there in the city.

The Church will be Built

Do you want to see the church in practical expression on earth in our day? Do you want to see the testimony of the Lord recovered and restored? Do you want to see God's original thought and concept— not merely thoughts and concepts—but factual reality? Do you want to see the glory of the latter house exceed that of the former? Then we must face it; the cost is all inclusive. All that you and I are must be brought to the cross as, to the altar, a living sacrifice. It means the *end* of what we are and what we want that He might have what He wants so that He may bring in what is of Himself and establish it. We have got to know what it is to be rent, to be broken, to be reduced to ashes, to fall into the ground and die, to decrease if *He* is going to increase and multiply and be glorified and exalted.

Do you want merely the success and prosperity of your own home, of your own career, of your own circle? Is it only your own spiritual growth, fullness and satisfaction that you seek? Are we content to centre everything in our own ceiled houses while the house of God lies waste and in ruin? Do we want position? Do we want ministry? Do we want comfort? Do we want friendship? Do we want fellowship? Do we want popularity? Then we must go our own way—good-bye. The house of God will never be rebuilt by such. That is the very reason that for so long it has lain waste. No, if we would see the house of God rebuilt we must face and accept the cost and by the grace of God never go back on it. It will be rebuilt in the measure in which you and I die.

Now, that is no comforting message unless you have faith in your heart. That is the message that came to the people when they went back to the land—blood, toil, sweat. You have to lay down your lives. But this is your glory! You shall have an everlasting name. You will be instrumental in bringing the Messiah back. You will be instrumental in the purposes of God, even if it may seem so ordinary and hum-drum with all the routine. You will be the precious material out of which God will build His city which will be forever and ever and in whose light the nations shall walk.

I tell you this that the house must be built. No matter if I die tonight or you die tonight, no matter if everyone of us become apostate this night, no matter what happens, the house of God is going to be built. It will be built whether you are in it or not, whether I am in it or not. We can say that with absolute and dogmatic certainty.

We have seen enough in world history to see that God *never* forsakes His purpose. We have seen miracles worked before our eyes. Do you think that the thing that lies nearest to the heart of God, more near than anything else to His heart, is not going to be fulfilled? Do you think that He can take back an earthly people to a place, a plot of ground on the earth according to His Word which He promised thousands and thousands of years ago and not fulfil this other thing which has lain on His heart from before time eternal and gives significance to eternity to come? No! The house of God is going to be built; it must be built. The top stone will be brought forth one day with shouts of "Grace, grace to it."

I pray God that I may be there. I pray God that you might be there. Wouldn't it be wonderful if we were all there to see the top stone slide into its place and to know that we are not spectators but part of it? Oh, my friend, I would rather go through hell to be in that than bang a tambourine for the rest of this time and dance to glory. I would rather be in the city. I had rather have gone into hell itself with Him and come out in eternal values. It will be accomplished and it will be fulfilled, not by might nor by power but by My Spirit, says the Lord of hosts. Just as the mountains stand round about Jerusalem as a perpetual reminder of the faithfulness of God, just as the sun shines by day and the moon shines by night, it is a perpetual reminder of the faithfulness of God. Just as the the rainbow in the day of storm and trouble, is a perpetual reminder of the faithfulness of God, just as these things will last throughout time, so will God be faithful to complete His purpose and will to do it. May God give us grace to come to the altar that the Holy Spirit may fall upon us. The word of the Lord is this: he that seeks My glory, to that one will I give My power and fill with My Spirit. Lord, hasten it in its time.

Let's pray, shall we?

Now Lord, there is not one of us that does not shrink from anything like an altar. We would much prefer, Lord, to just know that light-hearted and carefree existence. Lord, we know that Thou art seeking for those that will be good soldiers of Thine and we pray together that Thou by Thy Spirit will give every man and woman in this place faith; faith to die so that the Holy Spirit can commit Himself in an unparalleled way to every one of us. Oh, Father, Thou knowest our need of Thy Holy Spirit, our need of His power, our need of His fullness, our need of His dynamic, His impetus. Dear Lord, we look to Thee since Thou art the One who watches over all things and knows all things, that Thou wilt in Thy mercy bring every single one of us to the place where we are prepared to come to Thee as a living sacrifice, holy, acceptable unto Thee. We ask it together in the name of our Lord Jesus Christ. Amen.

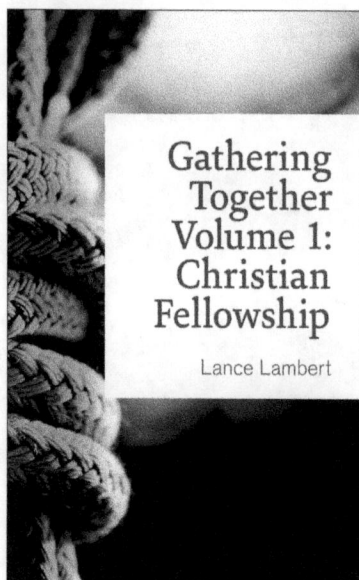

Gathering
Together
Volume 1:
Christian
Fellowship

Lance Lambert

Gathering Together

What is the church?

What is the basis for meeting together as the church?

What is true fellowship?

What is the priesthood of all believers?

What is the difference between unity
and uniformity in the church?

In this book, the first volume of *Gathering Together*, Lance
Lambert answers these questions and many more. In doing this,
he emphasizes the absolute headship of Christ and the oneness of
the body of Christ.

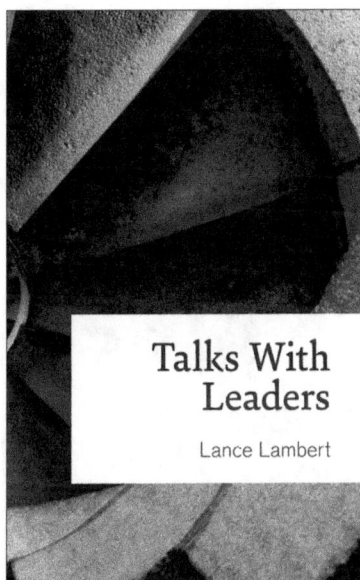

Talks With
Leaders

Lance Lambert

Talks With Leaders

"O Timothy, guard that which is committed unto thee ..."
(1 Timothy 6:20) Has God given you something? Has God
deposited something in you? Is there something of Himself
which He has given to you to contribute to the people of God?
Guard it. Guard that vision which He has given you. Guard that
understanding that He has so mercifully granted to you. Guard
that experience which He has given that it does not evaporate or
drain away or become a cause of pride. Guard that which the Lord
has given to you by the Holy Spirit. In these heart-to-heart talks
with leaders Lance Lambert covers such topics as the character
of God's servants, the way to serve, the importance of anointing,
and hearing God's voice. Let us consider together how to remain
faithful with what has been entrusted to us.

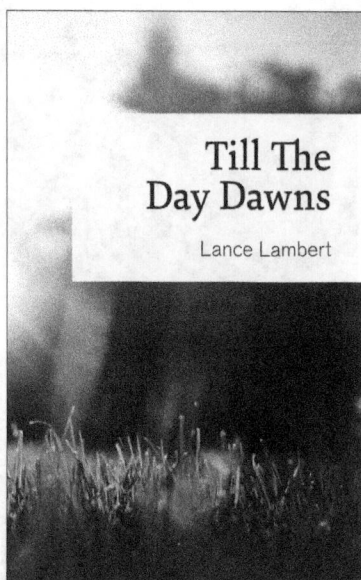

Till the Day Dawns

"And we have the word of prophecy made more sure; whereunto ye do well that ye take heed, as unto a lamp shining in a dark place, until the day dawn, and the day-star arise in your hearts." (II Peter 1:9).

The word of prophecy was not given that we might merely be comforted but that we would be prepared and made ready. Let us look into the Word of God together, searching out the prophecies, that the Day-Star arise in our hearts until the Day dawns.

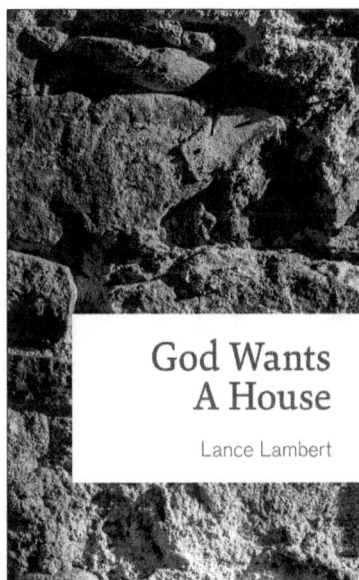

God Wants
A House

Lance Lambert

God Wants A House

Where is God at home? Is He at home in Richmond, VA? Is He at home in Washington? Is He at home in Richmond, Surrey? Is He at home in these other places? Where is God at home? There are thousands of living stones, many, many dear believers with real experience of the Lord, but where has the ark come home? Where are the staves being lengthened that God has finally come home? In *God Wants a House* Lance looks into this desire of the Lord, this desire He has to dwell with His people. What would this dwelling look like? Let's seek the Lord, that we can say with David, "One thing have I asked of Jehovah, that will I seek after: that I may dwell in the house of Jehovah all the days of my life, To behold the beauty of Jehovah, And to inquire in his temple."